DON'T FENCE ME IN!

by Barry Spanjaard
An American Teenager In the Holocaust

First Printing.................September 1981

Fifteenth Printing.................December 1993

Library of Congress Catalog Card No.: 81-68713

Spanjaard, Barry "Don't Fence Me In"
An American Teenager in the Holocaust.

Los Angeles, Ca. B & B Publishing

ISBN 0-9607008-0-3

FOR ORDERING INFORMATION AND LECTURE SCHEDULING, SEE PAGE 208

B. & B. PUBLISHING
P.O. Box 800165
Santa Clarita, California 91380
TEL (805) 255-3422
FAX (805) 254-1404

Printed By Delta Lithograph • Valencia, CA

THIS BOOK IS DEDICATED TO:

All the survivors who were prisoners
    of the Nazis during World War II
My dad, whom I loved dearly, and still miss
My mother, who didn't have an easy life
My wife Bunnie, who is my life, and who
    urged and helped me finish this book
    after 34 years
The 11 million (6 million Jews and 5 million
    non-Jews) who were viciously slaughtered
    by the Nazis
My grandmother, who was gassed in Sobibor,
    Poland
The Swiss Consul, the U.S. Department of
    State and the International Red Cross
    through whose efforts on my behalf I
    am still alive
The Jewish Community of Muensterlingen,
    Switzerland, for giving my dad a
    decent burial
Father John Neiman, who is my closest friend
    and adviser. He truly represents
    "ecumenical" in his life with his example
    of love, intelligence, understanding and
    generosity to me and all whose lives
    he touches
The thousands of students who have
    listened to my story in countless schools
    and have enriched my life with their
    love and attention
Fred Astaire.

We are extremely grateful to a young, very talented artist and good friend, David Pacheco. He drew, not only with his hand, but with his heart, the cover and the scenes from my life.

"I think the book is extremely well written and moved me very much. It gives people who have not known what happened in the concentration camps a very good picture of how people had to suffer under the Nazis...Anne only talks about the hiding.

I could identify with many things and could imagine how he felt when he was taken away, as he thought being American, he was safe.

I was very touched and astonished that a boy who lived near us, the same age as Anne Frank, has written of the time he was in the concentration camps."

Mrs. Otto "Fritzi" Frank

Basel, Switzerland

September, 1983

INTRODUCTION

When I re-read this almost forgotten memoir, I at first felt that this was another person, at another place, at another time...... It happened to someone else, not me. However, as I got into the story more in depth, most of it came back to me; things I had forgotten, or chose to forget.

I am so thankful to that young boy, myself at sixteen, who still had the advantage of recalling the events the middle-aged man, myself at fifty had forgotten.

It was quite painful to live through these experiences again, to feel the hunger, pain; and worst of all, the agonizing loss of my wonderful father. I grieved again, but I hope not in vain, for this may in some small way educate the young people of today as to what some young people of yesterday had to endure so that it may never happen again.

The author.

Fourth grade class picture, Amsterdam 1939. Of fifteen Jewish children (author circled), only THREE survived. Photo courtesy of Cora Mulder Harschel (girl in back row with ribbon in hair).

PROLOGUE

This is not a great literary project; it is simply the memoirs of Barry Spanjaard, written in a Virginia Military school in 1946, when he was supposed to be doing his homework. He was just sixteen years old. His teachers and roommates didn't know what he was writing. Barry simply sat down, and the words poured out of him in a torrent.

His "secret" project was to put down on paper his recent recollections of his family's experiences. What his schoolmates and teachers didn't know was that he had returned to the United States less than a year before; he was a survivor of Bergen-Belsen. That was his "secret," and he did a great job of hiding his past for many years.

Why the big secret? Was he ashamed? Was he so used to anti-semitism that he forced himself to assimilate so well, no one would suspect? Did he want to avoid pity? What propelled him to write his experiences down? This was 1946, and the world, as well as Barry, wanted to forget.

Psychologists may have the answer.... Releasing these tragic experiences may have been an act of self-therapy; since he couldn't or wouldn't talk about it, he *could* write about it.

When I met Barry in 1971, it was love at first sight. During our courtship, we went through the usual question and answer game. He told me he was born in New York City, was Jewish, divorced, and I enjoyed his wit and intelligence. We had so much in common; as I am also Jewish, born in the East, divorced, and we shared so many ideas and dreams.

After about six months, I asked him about his parents and his childhood. He suddenly became secretive, but I persisted—there was something he was hiding. When he casually mentioned he had moved to Holland at age two with his parents, and had returned to the United States at age fifteen, I did some arithmetic in my head and "brilliantly" said, "My God, you must have been in Europe during the war. You're Jewish, what happened to you?" He mumbled some reply about Bergen-Belsen, and I couldn't believe my ears.

I had read "The Diary of Anne Frank" and many other accounts of that period, and seen pictures of the atrocities at Belsen. My mother always admonished me as a child not to waste food, as "children in Europe are starving." Here I was, not only face to face with one of them, but I was deeply in love. I couldn't reconcile my image of Barry with the picture in my mind of the typical survivor, whatever that was. I started to question him further, but soon realized that he didn't want to talk about it.

We married in 1974, and travelled throughout Europe during 1975 and 1976, and during our visit to the Anne Frank House in Amsterdam, he suddenly opened up to me. He finally could talk about it. In fact, he told me he had it all written down, but didn't know where it was.

When we returned to the U.S., we looked, but couldn't find it. In the fall of 1978, we found the story, packed at the bottom of a carton we had put in storage. Barry spent the next few days reading it aloud to me. We laughed some, but mostly cried. For the first time he was sharing a part of his life he had shared with no one before. In the back of my mind, I also thought that this was "one hell of a story."

I managed to persuade Barry to work on it, and promised to help him. My writing style is more sophisticated than his, but at Barry's urging, the refining of the original is basically the same as he wrote it in 1946, through the eyes of a sixteen year old boy who had just learned English. All we have done is correct the spelling and punctuation. Needless to say, I wanted to make it a bit more polished, but Barry persevered, and I now know he was right.

So here it is, flaws and all, the story of my beloved's survival......

Bunnie Jurmain Spanjaard
Editor

1. FIVE DAY WAR DIARY

AMSTERDAM, HOLLAND, MAY 10th, 1940....As I woke up on this beautiful spring morning, I heard a lot of noise, louder than the noises I usually heard in the backyards in the morning made by women who were beating their rugs and doing other household chores. I looked at the time and saw that it was only 5 o'clock. Never before had I been awakened this early. I knew there was something wrong, and there was!

I heard my father and mother in the living room talking to our neighbors. Their voices sounded different. So I put on my bedroom slippers and went into the living room, not realizing that at that moment I was about to begin the most incredible five years of my life.

I was only ten years old, too young to understand fully what was happening. My father and mother tried to explain to me, in a way I could understand, what awful thing had happened a few hours before: Germany had, without warning, invaded our beloved Holland.

After getting dressed, I left the house. I found all my friends in the street. Everyone was looking up at the sky with worried looks on their faces. I looked up, and saw hundreds of German planes. The Dutch army, although very small, was trying with all its might to knock them out of the air with their artillery. The shells were exploding high in the sky, leaving many small smoke clouds behind. We were all very frightened, and yet it was exciting to watch.

After two hours, I decided to go up and have some breakfast, and heard my father listening to the radio for the
news. By this time everyone knew what was going on, but
maybe there would be something we hadn't heard yet. And
there it was! We were officially at war with Germany.

My father had belonged to the National Guard for many
years, and was called to report to their headquarters in
Amsterdam immediately. He put on his uniform, kissed my
mother and me goodbye, and left to report for duty. We kept
our radios on all that day in the hope of catching some of
the latest news, hoping for some good news.

Not long after my father had left, the mailman rang our
doorbell. He had a Special Delivery letter for me from the
American Consul. My mother opened it for me: it was the
most important letter I had ever received in my short ten
years. The Consul advised me, in fact urged me, to go back
to the United States that day. I was to report to a certain
place at 2 o'clock in the morning where a plane would be
waiting for the trip to the United States. But...., and here
is a very important BUT, I would have to go alone. My
parents could not go with me, because they were not American citizens, and I was. Just put yourself in my or my
parents' position for a few moments. Should they send me
to America alone? True, I had relatives there, but they were
strangers to me. It was a tough moment for the two of us,
as my father was on active duty, and my mother didn't
know whether to say yes or no. But as young as I was, I
decided to stay with my father and mother in my own
home, and stick it out with them along with all the other
Dutch people.

I couldn't picture being separated from my mommy and
especially my daddy, not knowing what would happen to
them. Not realizing it at the time, it turned out that I had
made the right decision. Had I gone to America, my parents would have been left in occupied Holland without the
protection of my American citizenship. The Nazis would
have shipped them off to Auschwitz in Poland and certain
death in the gas chambers. I would have felt responsible
for their deaths, something I would have had to live with

2

for the rest of my life. Surely, by remaining in Holland, I too had to suffer for many years; in fact still do, but at least I saved my mother's life, and got to spend another four years with my father. What a decision for a ten year old child to be faced with!

In the meantime, the radio announcer was still talking, so we sat down to listen. Time and again we heard him say, "Approximately 500 German paratroopers have just landed near Arnhem. Dutch troops managed to capture most of them." Then he would warn us about spies, about German soldiers dressed in civilian clothes. Many of them parachuted from planes dressed as women, preachers, and farmers. It was also announced that there was much sabotage; many of our planes and tanks had been found with sand in their gasoline tanks. We were warned about false radio broadcasts. Holland had only three radio news reporters, which was enough for a small country such as ours. It was reported that the Germans paid Dutch Nazi sympathizers to make radio broadcasts, in order to misinform the Dutch population.

We were also ordered to black out our windows and put tape on them, in case of a bombardment, so they wouldn't shatter. There were no lights at all on the streets at night; people weren't even allowed to smoke, as that too could be seen by enemy aircraft.

The rest of that day we had four or five air-raids, but nothing was damaged in Amsterdam. My father did not come home that night.

MAY 11th: I woke up very tired, because of the air alarms during the night. My mother and I had been awakened by the noise of the many planes, artillery fire and air raid sirens.

We immediately turned on our radio. Paratroopers were still coming down by the hundreds, the German ground troops were moving into Holland and were moving deeper into this beautiful peace-loving lowland. It was getting worse by the hour, even by the minute and second. We began to fear the worst.

It was getting so bad that some people, who were too

weak to face the future, committed suicide. The neighborhood doctor, Dr. M., gave his wife, mother-in-law and daughter a heavy dose of poison. Then he slashed his wrists and died within a few minutes.

The radio advised not to go too far away from our homes, in case of an emergency. I went to school, like any other day, but before classes started, a messenger entered with a personal message from the mayor of Amsterdam, telling all the students to leave and return to their homes immediately. I went home, but returned to the school a few hours later to see what was going on. The Dutch army had changed it into a hospital. That was the end of our school, at least for some time.

That day I received another official letter from the American consul urging me again to leave the country, and again I decided to remain in Holland as long as I could.

We went to visit some of our friends in the neighborhood. While we were there, my father had come home to get our radio so he and the other men could get the latest news where they were posted. We heard that he had been put in charge of the largest ammunition depot in Amsterdam, but he didn't tell us that, as we would have worried. It would be the first place the Germans would attack. My mother and I returned home and the neighbors told us that my father had been home and had left just a few minutes earlier. They had told my father about the letters I had received from the American consul. Dad left a note saying that he thought it would be a good idea for me to go to America. He also said goodbye. It seems that everyone agreed that I should leave; my mother, my father, our friends, the neighbors. I remained stubborn. How could I say goodbye to my dad, a man I loved so much, on a simple piece of paper?

MAY 12th: Another day of war, another day of uncertainty, air raids, bad news on the radio. That afternoon, my father came home, complete with rifle and helmet, prepared for battle. My mother and I asked him what work he did. He told us he had to guard a telephone communication center, as the army had taken it over. We went along with his deception, but we knew better, as our neighbors had

4

told us the truth. It occurred to me that this was Mother's Day, but there was nothing to celebrate for the mothers of Holland.

MAY 13th: The war was getting closer. Some paratroopers landed not far from my house. It started a panic, but soon it quieted down, after we were assured that the soldiers had been captured. Rotterdam really suffered that day. The entire business section of that beautiful city was completely destroyed, including hospitals, churches and homes. Thousands of people were killed.

This was the day the Royal family of Holland, Queen Wilhelmina, Princess Juliana, Prince Bernhard (a former German), and Princess Beatrix, saw it necessary to escape to England. They had to be extremely careful, as there were many spies in our midst, and the Queen dressed in farmer's clothes. The Dutch population did not like her leaving at all; feeling abandoned. Soon we realized it was necessary. If she had remained in Holland, as our surrender to Germany was inevitable, then Hitler would have possessed all of Holland's overseas territories as well, such as Indonesia, Surinam, Curacao, and Aruba.

MAY 14th: This is the day no Dutchman of my generation will ever forget; the day we were forced to surrender to the Germans. The Germans threatened Amsterdam, this beautiful old city, with the same destruction they had done to Rotterdam. In fact, a large amount of bombers were already on their way.

General Winkelman, in charge of the army, did the surrendering. That was a sad day. My dad phoned us that afternoon, and told us to leave quickly, as Amsterdam was in great danger. He suggested we go to my grandmother, who lived in Bloemendaal, a pretty suburb of Haarlem, 15 miles outside of Amsterdam. We arrived at my grandmother's at 5 o'clock that afternoon.

My grandmother, or "Oma" as I called her, had a room with a family in a private house, and we were told that she had left with my aunt and uncle to try an escape by boat to England. When they reached the harbor city of Ijmuiden, the last ship was ready to leave, but was already overloaded, and there was no room for them. My aunt and uncle had three children: one daughter in Australia, a son in New York, and one son at home who was studying to become a doctor.

He later went into hiding, was caught, sent to Auschwitz, and miraculously escaped by pretending to be dead after he and thousands of others had been machine-gunned by the guards during the final days of the war. He lay in the snow for three days, until it was safe for him to move, and got away. His parents were gassed.

About that time the news reached us; we had officially surrendered. My mother and I met a man with a car who was kind enough to take us back to Amsterdam. That night I witnessed something very disturbing: I saw men weep. When you see a woman cry, it is bad, but only half as bad as when you see a soldier throw down his rifle, lay down wherever he can find room, and just cry.

We finally arrived in Amsterdam and went straight to the headquarters of the Dutch National Guard. We had heard that all the men were being dismissed that night. When we reached there, again we saw men crying. In the crowd we finally found my father. It was obvious that he was terribly upset; his beloved Holland had been forced to fall to the Germans. It was good to see him and to know he was still alive, and we went home.

Over the roofs of the houses we could see a large black smoke cloud and a huge fire. The Dutch army had set fire to the largest gasoline tank, which was located right outside the city, so that the Germans wouldn't get it. It burned for about three days; no one could stop it.

At least one thing had changed for the better; all the lights were on again, but for only one night. The next night we had to sit and walk in the dark again. That night, and many more to come.

II. BACK TO THE OLD WORLD

My paternal family emigrated to the Netherlands in 1492, because they had been expelled from Spain during the Spanish Inquisition, as they were Sephardic Jews. According to my family tree, a Salomon Jacob, took the family name "Spanjaard" in 1812, which in Dutch means "Spaniard," or "one who comes from Spain." He had 13 children, of which 4 died at birth. My father is descended from the 9th surviving child.

On July 28th, 1903, an only child, a son, was born to Elizeba Groen and Barend Spanjaard, in Amsterdam, Holland. They named him Alfred Bernard Spanjaard. After completing his studies in 1922, his mother sent him to New York to find and marry a rich American Jewish girl. She had in mind one girl of Dutch ancestry whose father owned a large department store in New Jersey.

On November 30th, 1901, Wilhelmina Souget and Natan Levy Roozeboom, became the parents of twin girls, Berta and Abigael, also in Amsterdam, Holland. This would normally bring joy to any family, but not this one. Some years before, Natan Roozeboom had been the owner of a successful wholesale plumbing supply business. Because of setbacks and his heavy drinking, he lost his business. By the time the twins were born, the family was extremely poor, and already had three other children, Louis, Maurice and Rozette.

Abigael was not the favorite of the twins. Bep, as she

7

was always called, was the pretty one with all the personality, the one everyone liked. Abigael, who soon took the name "Sophie," was not as good-looking, rather heavy, and was made to feel unwanted.

So, when Sophie turned 19, she decided to go to the "new world," America, to take a chance on a fresh and improved life. She travelled "steerage" as many European immigrants had before her. She truly loved New York City, her new home, and the United States, which was so different from her life in Holland.

She soon learned to speak English fluently, and got a job as a store detective in Macy's Department Store. She was happily Americanized, and had no intention of returning to Holland. One night, she went to a Chinese restaurant, wearing a "flapper" style dress, complete with fringes. It was bitterly cold, so when she got there, she stood in front of a gas-burning stove in order to warm up. Her dress caught fire, and she was burned over a large part of her body.

A young man, also having dinner in this restaurant, immediately grabbed his overcoat and covered her flaming dress, putting out the fire. As the result of his quick action, she was saved and left with slight scars. This young man's name was (Alfred) "Fred" Spanjaard, and also a Dutch immigrant. They started dating, fell in love, and in 1926 became engaged.

When Fred's mother in Holland heard about this, she became very upset. So upset, in fact, that she took the first available ship to New York to prevent the marriage. In her mind, Sophie was low-class (poor), and not good enough for her one and only son. This was not part of her plan, as she had not sent her son such a great distance only to end up with a "common" Dutch girl. True love won out, and on Halloween Day, 1927, Fred and Sophie were married. This was the first time Fred had ever stood up to his mother, and as a result, Sophie's mother-in-law never accepted her into the family, causing many unpleasant incidents in the years to come.

The added feature to this marriage was when I arrived

8

on the scene on August 16th, 1929, at Polyclinic Hospital, in New York City. At my mother's urging, I was given the typical American name "Barry." A few weeks after my birth, the depression started, resulting in mass unemployment and tremendous poverty, here as well as all over the world. My father had to support a wife and child, and, unwillingly, took a job with his uncle, who was in the diamond business, or rather in the diamond smuggling business, although my father was not aware of it then. One day, this uncle, upon arriving in New York from a boat trip from Europe, had a porter carry some paintings to a waiting car. Suddenly, the porter dropped one, the frame broke, and diamonds rolled all over the pier. He was arrested, and after a trial, was given the choice of a $200,000 fine, or 20 years in prison. He chose to pay the fine.

My father, whose mind was more on artistic endeavors, such as art and music, rather than on business, would play his cello. His uncle couldn't understand this, and finally, in a fit of temper, broke the cello over my father's head. Needless to say, this was the end of their business relationship.

After that my dad had various jobs in the banquet departments of the Plaza Hotel and the Waldorf Astoria, where he worked directly under the world-famous chef, "Oscar of the Waldorf."

My parents were hardly making it financially, and his fondest wish was to return to Holland. He never adjusted to life in America, which he felt was based on the pursuit of the "almighty" dollar.

His wish came true when he received a telegram in 1932, stating that his father was gravely ill, was not expected to live, and would we please return to Holland to be at his bedside and take over his antique business.

My mother was against the idea of leaving her adopted country, which she had grown to love. In fact, she had started to study for her American citizenship. She also was not too crazy about the prospect of being so close to her mother-in-law, knowing how she felt about her. But in those days it was a wife's duty to go wherever her husband went. This was around the time that a man named Hitler

9

was making a name for himself, but most people didn't take him seriously.

My parents went to the Dutch Consul to apply for their new passports for the trip to Holland. Each passport cost $5, which was difficult for them to afford. The boat tickets for our journey to Holland had been paid for by my grandparents. The Dutch Consul, trying to be helpful in saving them $5, told my parents not to bother with a separate American passport for me. After all, I was only two years old, and there would be no problem putting me on my mother's Dutch passport. This rather insignificant action was to have tragic results in the years to come.

So, we left New York, and arrived in Amsterdam a few days later. My mother's father was waiting for us, and even though he had not seen his daughter in 12 years, and had never met my father or me, he grabbed me from my mother's arms. As he was an Orthodox Jew, he immediately took me to the men's room, pulled down my pants, and inspected to see if I had been circumcised. I am told that I then promptly urinated on his shoes, to show him that it was in good working order.

Not long after our arrival, my father's father passed away, and the three of us settled down to our new life in the old country. I was 2½ years old, and spoke English like any other "red-blooded" American boy that age. (Even though I was now living in Europe, the color of my blood did not change.) In a short time I learned to speak Dutch, and completely forgot my English. My mother wanted to continue speaking English at home so I would not forget my native tongue; but my father insisted that we speak the language of the country in which we were residing, so Dutch it was. This then became our permanent home, at least for the next eleven years.

We lived in a middle class modern section of Amsterdam; not at all like the old, but charming, inner city. Our apartment faced a canal, which ran into a larger river, called De Amstel, which was on the corner of our street. Amsterdam got its name from this canal. It was originally called Amsteldam (dam on the Amstel), but over the years it became known as Amsterdam.

From the second floor, although in the United States it would be called the third floor, we had a beautiful view from large picture windows in our living and dining rooms. I had my own bedroom in the rear of the apartment, next to which on one side was the kitchen and on the other side my parents' bedroom. We had an old fashioned W.C. (water closet), which is all that it was; just a toilet—no bathtub or shower, only the rich people had them. Upstairs, above the third floor, was the attic where we had an additional two rooms used for storage.

Above us lived a young married couple who became our friends. However, after the Nazis occupied Holland, we discovered that he was a member of the Dutch Nazi Party, the N.S.B. Below us was an older couple who had lived in Holland for many years after leaving their native Germany, Mr. and Mrs. O. and her elderly mother. After the German occupation, Mr. and Mrs. O. were obliged to open their home to German officers. Every Sunday night there would be about ten of them, usually getting drunk and singing German bar songs, which made us feel very uncomfortable. The next day, Mrs. O. would apologize to us, hoping that it didn't bother us; explaining they really didn't want to play hosts, but had no choice.

A Jewish family also lived in our building with a lovely daughter, Nannie, who was two years older than me. This was my first romance. She was quite aggressive, and would suggest all kinds of games to play; "house," "doctor and nurse" and we would reverse roles. Other neighbors were Mr. and Mrs. v.d.L. My parents told me I mustn't talk to them as they belonged to the Communist Party, a feared political organization.

The building we lived in was a small part of a large quadrangle, a four story structure which went around the block and faced four different streets. Within this block was most of my world; my friends, the grocery store, milk and cheese store (Oome Kees), vegetable store (Tante Naatje), and the neighborhood bicycle shop. We did not have an icebox, as this was only for the well-to-do, so our food was delivered daily to our door, such as bread, milk, and fish. We even had a pickle man who came every Friday. Our news-

11

paper, De Telegraaf, was delivered by a grown man, as it was his job; boys didn't deliver papers, as they do in America.

Holland moved almost entirely by bicycle; there were very few cars. The only people I knew who had a car were our German neighbors downstairs, because he was in the car business. My father had a bike, and went everywhere with it. When he had to go out of town on business, he would ride it to the railroad station and put it on the train; take it off when he got to his destination, and pedal to the people he had to see. He was a bicycle enthusiast. He belonged to the Dutch bicycle club (A.N.W.B.), and went on many bicycle trips, for which he received many medals.

I didn't own a bike, and really didn't need one, as everything I needed was right in our neighborhood, including school, which was only about a ten minute walk. My parents couldn't afford to buy me one. When I was small, my father would take me places with him on his bike in a small basket he had attached to the package carrier in back. I saw the entire city of Amsterdam from this position. When I got old enough to learn how to ride a bicycle, my Father would occasionally rent one for me from the shop around the corner. This was where he stored his bike every night and had all the repairs done. Renting a bike was 10 cents an hour, not a small amount in those days, so I knew how to ride a bike, but still didn't have one.

There was no way a young boy my age could earn any money. I didn't get any allowance; it was still the depression and I remember my father and mother having discussions where the money would come from for tomorrow's food. Our rent was 35 guilders, which was about 10 dollars American money. A few years later my grandmother gave me 3 cents a week allowance, and I would go to the candy store and load up. Every once in a while, a family friend or distant relative would visit us, and would give me a nickel or a dime. I would run downstairs and show all my friends, and I would be the "king" of the entire neighborhood.

To show the poverty that existed in those days, there were "schillenboers" (peel farmers). The Dutch are great potato eaters, and these men would come through the neighborhood with their horses and wagons collecting potato peels, which they would sell to the farmers to feed their pigs.

So, where would I be able to get the money to rent a bicycle, something I wanted so much? I finally found the answer; my father had a habit of putting his keys, wallet, and change on a table in his bedroom. I would sneak in early in the morning, and without waking him up, steal a dime from the table; and after school, would rent a bike. This went well for a while, until one night when my father brought his bike to the shop for his regular overnight storage. The owner told my father what a good customer I was, and that I had become a good rider.

My mother took me to the juvenile police, and I was taken into a huge grey building and led into a dark room. Two men talked to me, and told me that if I didn't stop stealing they would lock me up. They scared the hell out of me. I came out shaking and crying. It must have made a big impression on me, as I never stole anything else again. The worst of it was that I had greatly disappointed my daddy, who was my idol.

I still called my father "daddy," a habit I had taken with me from America, which my Dutch friends could never understand; they thought I was calling him by his first name. That, and the fact that I had dark, olive-colored skin and curly, dark blond hair, unlike most of the Dutch people who have straight blond hair, was the reason I was given the nickname: "Afrikaanse Bos Neger," (African bush negro).

Our life until that fateful day, May 10, 1940, was very much like any other Dutch family. Daddy took over his father's antique brokerage business, and was known in Dutch as a "makelaar," which is a middle-man who represents wealthy art and antique collectors at auctions, because of his ability to judge the quality and value of these items. His clients had complete trust in him, and more often than not, he would do the bidding and purchasing without the client being present. Friday, Saturday and Sunday was "kijkdagen," at which time the items to be sold would be displayed for prospective buyers. This was done in an attractive museum-like atmosphere. Many Sundays my mother and I would join my father there, and he would explain about rare paintings, Persian rugs, silver, sculpture and antique furniture. I often wonder if this war business hadn't happened, I would have gone into this profession with him.

Being as my father was in this business, our house was furnished with rare and expensive antiques, including a large collection of first-edition books. I was told that I was never to have anyone in the house unless my father or mother were home.

I attended the Jan Lievensschool, Smarachtplein #5,from 9 AM to 12 noon, then went home for lunch, returning at two until four. Twice a week, from 4:30 PM to 5:30, I took French lessons. This was not required, but my parents thought it was a good idea. We had no school on Wednesday afternoons, but went on Saturday mornings, when we would have an hour and a half of reading, and the rest of the morning would be spent on art.

On Wednesday afternoons, the housewives would go downtown to shop, mostly to windowshop. Their favorite place was De Kalverstraat, a street which had many small and large stores. Most of the time my mother would take me with her, something I disliked as I would have to wait for her for hours.

Some Wednesdays, every two years to be exact, it was different; we wouldn't go shopping. This would be the day my mother would take me to the American consul, to re-register me as an American citizen. I will be forever grateful to my mother for this. I am sure she was proud to be the parent of an American-born son, and it was always her secret desire to go back to America some day. It wasn't until some time later that we realized how important these little visits to the consulate had been. In fact, if she had not taken the time out to do this, I would have lost my American citizenship, and not be alive today.

Though my father's time was mostly taken up with business, he still managed to find time for other interests. He remained active in the Boy Scout movement, an organization he had been with since childhood; joined the Dutch National Guard; became a Big Brother to a fatherless little

14

boy; and became a licensed city lifeguard. There was need for my father to become a lifeguard, even though we lived 15 miles from the ocean. Amsterdam has many canals, and almost every day someone would fall into one of them.

Opposite our house was a grey boat in the canal, used by the city gardeners to store their tools. When I was six years old, this boat became my favorite playground. One afternoon, while playing "tag" there, I ran to get away from the boy who was "it," right into the water. I went down twice, with dirty brown water all around me, and panicked. I had heard if one couldn't swim and went down three times, that was it; he would not come up again. My playmates were yelling: "Help, help, a kid in the water!" Soon, a good samaritan ran to the scene. (All this time no sign of my father; who was, after all, an official lifeguard and lived no more than 50 feet from where his own son was drowning.) He hung over the side of the boat, and stuck out his leg to me. I grabbed it, and he pulled me out of the water. Here I was, sopping wet, half-drowned, trembling with fear; and who comes strolling by, calm as can be... but my own father, the official neighborhood lifeguard. He had been to the corner grocery store, heard a commotion and came to see what was going on. For some reason, my Dad now thought it was time for me to take swimming lessons, and the next day I found myself in the Heilige Weg indoor pool, learning how.

I never did know my grandmother on my mother's side, as she had died many years before. In the meantime, my "Oma" (my Dad's mother), never did accept my father and mother's marriage, and continued to make life miserable for my mother. She would nag my father over and over: "Why don't you leave that woman?" She loved my father and me, and did thoughtful and nice things for me, buy me clothes, invite me to spend weekends with her; and took me to visit relatives in Brussels, Belgium, which was a big thrill for me, as I had never really been anywhere. As for my mother, that was a different story. Mom never had much use for her either, and I could hardly blame her. I remember her saying, "Your grandmother is like a cow who gives good milk, and then kicks over the bucket."

Grandmother was instrumental in my parents not getting along, and this made for tension in our home. My father and mother were always arguing, particularly my mother with my father, mostly after I had gone to bed when she thought I couldn't hear. I couldn't sleep because of her yelling.

To me, all the man wanted after being out in the business world all day, was to be left alone. I would overhear him say, "Het enige wat ik wil, is rust en kalmte" (all I want is some peace and quiet). This built up resentment on my part towards my mother. Many nights I couldn't fall asleep because of the carryings on, and I constantly lived in fear that they would get divorced, and then what was to become of me? I envisioned my world falling apart.

My mother took me along with her once to a lawyer to discuss divorce, and I felt terrible. My Oma had almost succeeded in breaking them up.

In 1933, many German Jews who escaped from Germany to get away from Hitler, came to Holland. Among them were young girls in their late teens and early twenties who, after arriving in Holland had no place to go, so they were put in an orphanage. Dutch families hired some of these girls as live-in maids, and my parents did the same.

Our maid's name was Annie. She was attractive, had a nice figure, dark brown eyes and long black hair. Many of these girls, including Annie, were very ambitious and their goal was to change their role from "maid of the house" to "mistress of the house." The best way to do this was to seduce the "man of the house," and this Annie did. Here was this young girl, right there in his own house, so Dad succumbed to the temptation. My mother found out about it; and this made things even worse; the tension became almost unbearable.

My mother threatened to commit suicide. One morning, the milkman came to our house during his usual rounds of delivery, and when there was no answer to his knock on the door, he went in and found my mother with her head in the gas oven. I always suspected that her timing was just right. The milkman was coming, so she would be disco-

16

vered and saved. She then "went away for a while." To a rest home, I was told.

Annie, of course, was fired, got married, and shortly after that got divorced. She said she still was "in love" with my Dad, as he was a quiet, shy, attractive man, with a dry sense of humor, the type women go for. He had other lady friends, on occasion, but I don't think he instigated these affairs.

Dad was the athletic one; Mom, on the other hand, was just the opposite. However, he tried to get her interested in outdoor activities, and on occasional Sundays he would rent a tandem, put my little basket in the back, and the three of us would ride through Amsterdam. Because of its many canals, Amsterdam also had many steep bridges. My mother was always afraid to stay on the tandem while going over these bridges, so she would get off the bicycle, walk over the bridge, and we would wait for her on the other side. This cramped our style a bit. These family outings were more for my benefit.

As a rare treat, my Dad would take my mother to the movies to see "The Hunchback of Notre Dame" and "Pygmalion," which were dubbed into Dutch. Mother was a frustrated actress; and would have made a great one, as she was always very dramatic. When she came home from these movies, she would act out the entire plot for me.

Whenever my Dad wasn't working on weekends, he would put my little basket on the back of his bike and we would be off to Schiphol Airport, or the Zuider Zee, taking a picnic along. We would sit there together, watching the planes take off and land, and he would explain that these planes were on their way or coming from places all over the world. It was totally fascinating to me, and always will be. I am grateful for these precious moments I had with him.

He was a fine person, and highly respected in his profession by his colleagues, because of his honesty and integrity. That's probably why he never made any REAL money; whereas, many of his competitors were quite well-to-do. Mijnheer C.H. B. worked for my father many years as a delivery man. Whenever my father purchased an item at an auction for a client, Mijnheer B. would deliver it on his "bakfiets" (a three wheeled cycle with a large open flat bed to haul).

Other than my grandmother, "Oma" and my mother's father, "Opa", I had no close relatives in Holland. As my father was an only child, I had no aunts or uncles on his side. He had a few cousins, but they didn't have much to do with us, because of my grandmother's influence. I had some wealthy relatives, such as the Spanjaard family from Borne, who owned very large textile mills, but I never met them. There are relatives, on both my mother's and father's side, named Citroen. They had moved to France many years before, and manufactured cars, but not before they put ¨ over the "e" of Citroen. I don't blame them as Citroen in Dutch means lemon, not a good name for a car.

I was very envious of my friends whenever they would tell me they were going to visit their uncles and aunts, or cousins were coming to visit them. As I didn't have this, I always felt left out. Of course, I did have family, but they all lived in other countries. My mother had two brothers and two sisters. One brother, Louis, had moved to Paris, France many years before, married a French lady, Madeleine, and they had two sons, Roger, and Norbert. Another brother, Maurice, moved to New York before I was born and married an American girl named Cora. They had a daughter named Rita. My mother's twin sister, Bertha, or "Bep," married Jo, also in New York.

Uncle Jo came to visit us once, when he returned to Holland to attend his mother's funeral. He was the only close relative I had ever met from America, and I was most impressed. He had flown to Europe on a Pan American Clipper, on one of its first flights across the Atlantic Ocean. When he came to say goodbye to me, I started crying bitterly. My parents could not understand; after all, I had only met this man just a few days before. But I wanted to keep him with me to show my friends that I too had an uncle.

My mother's oldest sister, Rozette, or "Zeddie," many years before had met a Dutch boy named Jacques, who emigrated to the United States. She wanted to follow him, but her father, who was very religious, would not allow it unless she was married. She married Jacques by proxy, moved to New York, and they became the parents of Florence.

Looking back now, I really understand why my mother was so anxious to return to New York. Not only did she love that city, and the American way of life, but most of her close relatives were there.

My summer vacation from school was from mid-July until mid-August. We usually returned to school at the time of my birthday, August 16th. Amsterdam was hot and muggy in the summer, so my parents sent me to Zandvoort, a beach resort 20 miles from Amsterdam. I would stay in a so-called "kinderhuis," or children's home, which was run by a nurse, Zuster v.d.B. and her husband, who did all the cooking. I never wanted to go, and would have much preferred staying home with my father and friends. I would get very homesick and miss my Dad very much.

One morning when I was in the children's home, I must have done something wrong, I don't remember what. When we sat down at one large table for lunch, about 15 children and a few counselors, I was ordered to take off all my clothes in front of everyone, and go upstairs to my room. I was so embarrassed I wanted to die. I ran upstairs, flopped on my bed, crying hysterically: "I want my Daddy! I want my Daddy!" Soon, someone knocked on my door and said I should come downstairs right away and put on some clothes first, as I had a visitor. It was my Dad! I was so happy to see him that I ran up to him, jumped up and threw my arms and legs around him; I never wanted to let him go. He had just decided to come and visit me, and his timing couldn't have been better.

Mom and Dad courting,
New York City, 1925

Oma's visit to New
York, to stop Dad's wedding.

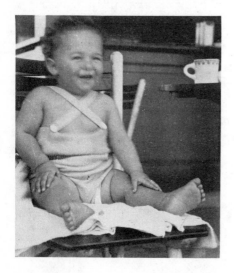

Baby Barry - U.S.A.

"Opa", me and Uncle Louis from Paris, December 12, 1933

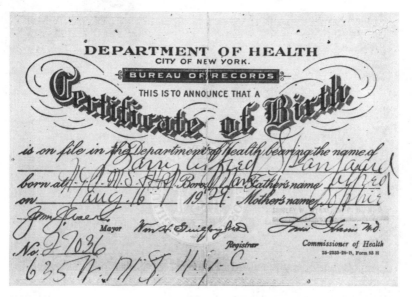

My only proof of American Citizenship

"Afrikaanse Bosneger" (on the right). Zandvoort, Holland, Summer 1936

Bloemendaal Deer Park, March, 1937

Daddy's favorite hobby; long distance bicycle tours, Sept., 1939

III. THOSE WERE THE DAYS

As an American-born child, living in Holland, I felt different; an outsider, always very intrigued about anything American. There was a popular song we heard on the radio, which people were singing or whistling on the street; "Bei Mihr Bist Du Schön," by the Andrews Sisters. It was thrilling for me to know that this came from America, and wanted to tell everyone that it had come from MY country.

It was big news in Holland when President Roosevelt spoke, which we picked up on our short-wave radios. He was looked upon not only as the President of the United States of America, but also as the most important leader in the world. We had learned in school that he was of Dutch descent. Whenever he spoke, very few people were on the streets. Even though I could not understand him, I could feel that it was important. My parents would translate for me that it had to do with whether or not there was going to be war. I had a picture of President Roosevelt on my bedroom wall. The face was made up of typical American sights, the Statue of Liberty, an oil well, the Empire State Building, the George Washington Bridge, the Grand Canyon, the White House. Under his picture was printed: "Eendracht maakt macht." (In unity there is strength.)

The world-famous boxer and heavy-weight champion, Joe Louis, also created a lot of excitement. Whenever he fought, everything stopped. I particularly remember the match he had with Max Schmeling, which was more than just a heavyweight fight. There were politics involved, and when Joe knocked out the German champion in the first round, I thought everybody was going crazy; people cheered, screamed and clapped their hands.

Another famous American was Shirley Temple. Since I had never been to the movies, I really didn't know who she was, except that she was very famous and a rich movie star. One day they announced a Shirley Temple look-alike contest, and my mother, for some reason, thought I was the spitting image of her. She had me pose for pictures in our dining room, and sent them in. I didn't win, although I never could figure out why.

Even though they were Canadian (to me it was still American), the Dionne quintuplets were extremely popular in Holland. The Palmolive Soap Co. had a big promotion for them. If you bought a certain amount of their soap, you got a coloring book of the quintuplets, complete with cut-out dresses. Though that wasn't the usual kind of toy for a boy, I was still happy about having one of those books.

One afternoon my mother took me to Carree, a large theatre in Amsterdam, because a "very famous" American singer named Jo Peterson, was appearing there, with publicity that he had the most beautiful voice in the world, and was the biggest singing star in the United States. Well, he had a beautiful voice and was a big hit in Holland, but some time later we found out that "he" was really a "she."

Every Monday morning in class, it was time to bring in "school geld" (school money). The public schools were not supported by taxes as they are in the United States. Each student had to bring in school money to pay for the school, according to the income of the family. The teacher would call out the names of each student in class, and collect this fee. It would go like this: "Felix, 3 cents—Max, 27 cents—Barry, 5 cents—Theo, 45 cents." The amount was based on the father's income, and we all knew who was poor and who was rich. What an embarrassing way to handle this.

Very little was known about child psychology in those days. One morning I was told by my parents they were going to take me for ice cream, and naturally, I was happy.

24

We went on the streetcar, and then I got suspicious; why go in the streetcar to get ice cream, when there was an ice cream store right in our neighborhood? Before I knew what was happening, I was taken to a doctor's office and brought upstairs. I was made to sit on a gorilla-looking man's lap, who was wearing a red rubber apron. He wrapped his arms and legs around me, told me to open my mouth wide. Someone held a large white dish under my chin, and my tonsils were removed. Blood gushed out, and I was terrified. The only good thing about this episode was that we went home in a taxi, a new experience for me. After we got home, I finally did get my ice cream. I never forgave my parents for this deception.

No one, except the very rich, had a shower or bathtub in their house, but there were public bath houses. I would walk about a mile to get to one of them, where for "een stuivertje" (a nickel) I took a shower. This was fine, except on cold winter days (there were plenty of them in Holland) when I had to walk home after a nice hot shower.

Living on a canal was pleasant and fun. First of all, it gave us a beautiful view from our windows. On hot summer afternoons, some of my friends and I would sneak in a swim, until someone came and chased us out. It was illegal to swim in the canals, as they were made for boats, not for swimming, the water was polluted. On Sundays people would pass by our house in their small yachts, and during the week the local rowing clubs would practice in their one, two, four and eight men skiffs.

During winter these canals would freeze, and we would go skating on them. Almost everyone had skates, Dutch style; wooden, with blades and straps to tie onto your shoes. I didn't have any, but a relative from New York sent me a pair of second-hand figure skates, with shoes attached. I was thrilled and felt rich, as few kids had shoe skates. The only problem was that they were about five sizes too large, and I didn't know how to skate. But this didn't stop me; first, I filled up the skates with wrinkled-up newspapers, and onto the ice I went, falling all over the place. The next day I took an old kitchen chair, put it in front of me and held on for dear life. Soon I learned to skate and became one of the better skaters in the neighborhood, particularly at speed skating. Men with hand-operated snow shovels came to push the snow out of the way to clear the ice, thereby creating a nice rink for the skaters. On the ice were stands where they sold hot chocolate, a delightful memory.

As I enjoyed skating so much, my Daddy bought me a pair of German roller skates. I'd never seen skates like that before, or since. They had two large rubber wheels in the front and one small one in the back, much like a small airplane. I had a lot of fun with them; I could even use them to skate on cobblestones, much to the envy of the kids in the neighborhood.

Another one of my favorite toys was a "Vliegende Hollander" (Flying Dutchman), which I have never seen in this country. It was like a soapbox on wheels. You'd steer it by placing your feet on the front axle, and it had a handle you would push and pull to make it go. There was enough room in the back for another person.

I often wonder what happened to these wonderful playthings of mine, as well as the beautiful things my parents had. The day after we were arrested, a large truck pulled up to our house, took everything out, and shipped it to Germany.

One summer, when my father had come to pick me up to take me home by train from my stay in Zandvoort, he asked me what I would like the most for my birthday, which was the next day. I told him what I wanted more than anything, a dog. He said to wish real hard for one, which I did, but never really thought it would work. Sure enough, when I arrived home, there was a beautiful dog, a German shepherd, whom I called "Teddy." I took him everywhere with me, and he would wait for me in front of the house when I was in school. But my mom was not too crazy about him, and on December 31st, she told me that Teddy was "sick" and had to be put away. It was one of the saddest days of my life.

Christmas is spent differently in Holland than it is in the United States. It is strictly a Christian Holy Day, celebrated on December 25th, when no gifts are exchanged. The gift-giving is done the night of December 4th, which is the birthday of St. Nickolas, or as he is called in Dutch, "Sinterklaas." Jews and Gentiles alike celebrate this occasion. The highlight of this festival is when "Sinterklaas" "arrives" from Spain, where he lives, with his black helpers (Zwarte Piet) by boat and all the kids are given the afternoon off from school to watch his arrival and there is much excitement. I have the feeling the reason he lives in Spain is that that climate is so much more pleasant than that of Holland, or for that matter, the North Pole, which is the U.S. tradition.

Every night for about a week, every child in Holland puts one of his shoes by the fireplace, together with a dish of water and some straw for Sinterklaas' horse. When we got up in the morning, the straw and the water were gone, and there would be a small present in the shoe, which meant he had been there. Then on December 5th, in the evening, we had "strooi avond" (the showering of gifts). This was always a happy time and one December in my Montessori kindergarten, when Sinterklaas was coming to our school, we were told that those of us who had been bad during the year, would get a spanking from one of Santa's helpers. This was usually done with a bunch of twigs that had been bundled and tied together. I probably had done something wrong during the year (who hadn't?) and got so nervous, I threw up.

One "strooiavond," after an endless wait for the big night, I had received no gifts and was sent to bed. My parents said: "Well, I guess Santa is not coming to visit you this year." I was so upset, I started to cry. On my way to bed, I heard a tremendous noise of doors slamming. I ran back into the living room, and to my delight, there was a burlap bag full of gifts. There were black fingerprints on the doors that Santa's helpers "had left there."

It was the following year when I was home for lunch from school, that my mother told me there was no "Sinterklaas." I refused to believe her; it had all been so real to me. Later on, when I did believe her, I resented that she had told me this when I was seven, instead of waiting a little longer until I was twenty or so.

The summer of 1937 was an exciting one in Holland, the year the International Boy Scout Jamboree was held in Vogelzang, a small town about 15 miles outside of Amsterdam. It was very fascinating for a boy my age (7), to see teenage boys from all over the world. Many came from countries I had never heard of. It became a contest among the youth of Holland to collect autographs from scouts from every country, and I gathered quite a few in my little yellow book. Some writings I could not read, as they were in Greek or Japanese, who had different alphabets.

Dad was very active in the Dutch Boy Scout movement, and spent the entire ten days at the Jamboree. Because of his ability to speak Dutch and English fluently, he was chosen to be the personal interpreter for Lord Baden Powell, the Englishman who founded the Boy Scout movement. I went several times and attended many of their impressive ceremonies. On one of my visits, Dad introduced me to Lord Baden Powell, and he took me to a big tent where they had Boy Scout accessories for sale, and bought me an official Boy Scout neckerchief slide. It wasn't until years later that I realized how important he was.

Every country in the world was represented at this event, much like the Olympics, with the exception of Germany, which had already outlawed the Boy Scouts and replaced it with the "Hitler Jugend" (Hitler Youth).

There was such warm feelings among all the different nationalities, everyone felt that with all this camaraderie, brotherhood and togetherness, it was unthinkable that these very same young men would EVER pick up arms to fight against each other..... how wrong they were!

IV. THE "MOFFEN" GET ROLLING

Two days after Holland's surrender to Germany, we were awakened by a loud, constant rumbling. Quickly I got dressed, and went outside to investigate. I noticed a large crowd had gathered at De Amsteldijk, a broad boulevard about 200 yards from my house. The German forces had taken its first of many steps. It seemed as if they were moving everything they had into Holland to show off their might, on their way to Belgium and France. And impressive it was! I saw trucks, cannons, cars, rolling kitchens, motorcycles, and tanks manned by the feared "Totskopfen Regiment." The skull and crossbones was their insignia, and they had sworn to give up their lives for Hitler.

They kept on rolling and rolling, the smell of diesel fuel in the air, the ground vibrating, for several days. It was so loud, we couldn't sleep at night.

Then the Grune Polizei (green police or German military police) entered the city in huge trucks, and took over the job of the Amsterdam Police. They knew the way, thanks to the Dutch Nazis, who had given them maps. These Nazi sympathizers were now standing on the street watching this parade and throwing flowers.

My friend, Gerard, was standing next to me. He was a gentile boy, the type Hitler liked: straight blond hair, and blue eyes, a typical Aryan. Suddenly, when the parade had come to a temporary halt, one of the soldiers jumped off his tank and approached my friend, asking him if he would

29

like to come and visit Germany. Gerard told him that he would like to very much; whereupon the soldier took his name and address.

A couple of weeks later, Gerard received an invitation, railroad tickets, and official travel papers, to go to Germany for two weeks. When he returned in the Hitler Youth uniform, he was a different person, and told me that he was no longer permitted to associate with me. His father was to become one of the important Nazis in the neighborhood. In spite of all this, his sister, Toby, a cute little blonde, was one of my girlfriends. She would walk one way and I would go the other so as not to be spotted, usually meeting at a construction site. We'd play "I'll show you mine if you show me yours" little sex games.

When Holland was liberated, she fell in love with an American Jewish soldier and she thought they were going to be married. But he jilted her, probably because he had found out about her family's Nazi affiliation. She then had a nervous breakdown and ended up in a mental institution.

The next step that occurred that made us fully realize that we were now living in an occupied country, was rationing. Holland has always been the land of plentiful butter, cheese, milk and eggs. When foreigners move in suddenly, create a shortage, tell you what you can eat and how much of it you are allowed, it is like another invasion. The Hollanders had no choice but to go along with this. But patriotism was in their blood; you can't ration that.

Queen Wilhelmina's birthday was August 31st. That night, the Dutch people were feeling very low. About nine o'clock in the evening, hundreds of British planes flew over Holland and threw out fire crackers in celebration of the Queen's birthday and to lift our morale. It was a beautiful sight, as everything around was in total darkness. We felt very good about it, but it made the "moffen" (our own slang word for the Germans) angry.

My grandfather, on my mother's side, was well in his eighties by this time. We would usually visit him every Sunday in a "pension" where he lived in the old Jewish section of Amsterdam. This was a boarding house with several other elderly people. His life consisted mostly of his daily visits to Artis, the Amsterdam Zoo, around the corner from the pension, where he had a life-time membership. He also enjoyed his "borrelen" (drinking), in fact, it was more than enjoyment; he couldn't live without it.

There was something else very important in his life. His favorite grandson, Norbert, who was from a little village outside of Paris, had been in the French Air Force during the recent war against Germany, and we had not been able to get any news about him; we didn't know if he was alive or dead.

Every time we visited my grandfather, the first thing he would ask was: "Have you heard anything about Norbert?" But our answer was always: "No, but don't worry, he is young and strong, and we are sure he is all right."

News about Norbert finally arrived on December 10th, 1940, almost seven months after the war in France, he was alive. My grandfather was overjoyed. That night, for the first night in a long time, he was able to fall asleep easily. And fall asleep he did... he never woke up... he died during the night, a happy man.

One of the first official actions against the Jews occurred on February 24th, 1941. I had gone to the Tip Top Theatre in the old Jewish section of Amsterdam. The Krauts made it their business to find out at what time the theatre would be filled. On this particular afternoon, the infamous Grune Polizei blocked off the entire theatre and the surrounding neighborhood, and went insde. The leader went backstage, and without knocking, went into one of the actress' dressing rooms. He ordered her to go on stage and announce that all Jewish men between the ages of 16 and 35 had to report in front of the theatre immediately. There was no way of escaping, the Germans had taken care of that. As the men came outside, they were told to put their hands up and behind their necks, and to keep them that way until they were told to do otherwise. These men were marched to a nearby square, Waterlooplein.

They were then ordered to crawl on their hands and knees

around the square for an hour. The Germans enjoyed this, as they stood there watching and laughing. I, thank God, didn't have to participate in this, because I was only twelve years old. But, just the sight of these men being humiliated was bad enough. About sixty men collapsed. After the rest were exhausted, they were pushed into large trucks, and taken away. Relatives of the kidnapped young men wrote to the Germans to ask if there was anything that could be done for them. They were told they could send them packages. After a few days of this, the Germans got tired of the whole business, and sent notices to the relatives informing them that the men had all died of some disease, and if they wished to have the ashes of their dead relatives sent to them, it would cost them 10 guilders in cash for each. Some people did, and then discovered that the ashes they received were not human ashes. The whole thing had been a hoax; after the war I met one of these "dead" men.

To the best of my knowledge, Jewish people in Holland had never experienced anti-Semitism, at least not before the war. The Gentile population, in order to show the Germans their regard for the Jews and what had happened on the day before, plus their dissatisfaction in general, went on strike February 25th. Everything stopped; the trains, streetcars, buses, telephone service, and banks were closed. But what could ten million well-meaning people do against a mighty army which was not afraid to use its weapons? All our weapons had been turned in one week after the occupation. Martial law was declared; no one was allowed in the streets after eight o'clock that night, more than two people on the street talking was considered a "meeting" and was not permitted. It was also announced on the radio and on billboards all over town that if the strike was not halted immediately, hostages would be taken. So, the next day it was all over, and the Dutch people were fined 15 million guilders for their heroic but fruitless action.

Princess Juliana, the daughter of Queen Wilhelmina, was married to a German prince, Bernhard, in 1937. It was his custom to wear a white carnation. His birthday is June 29th, and the Dutch wanted to do something special that

32

day, so they wore carnations, and paraded proudly along one of Amsterdam's busiest streets, De Kalverstraat, wearing them on their lapels. There were Nazis there, who tore the flowers from their coats. But some young college students had a bright idea, they put flowers on their lapels with something new added; sharp razor blades behind them. They returned to De Kalverstraat and many a Nazi finger was cut that day. (That left them a bit shorthanded.)

One night I was awakened by a tremendous explosion. Windows were broken all over the house, and pieces of shrapnel and earth were falling all over my bed. I jumped out of bed and ran into my parents' bedroom who were already awake. Dad suggested that we immediately go into the basement of the building. Still very frightened, we joined our other neighbors already there.

The next morning we found out what had happened. Around the corner from us was a small park, and a bomb had fallen in the middle of it, no more than 40 yards from my home. It was broadcasted on "Radio Oranje," an illegal Dutch radio station from England, that a British plane on its way to a bombing mission in Germany, had been hit by anti-aircraft artillery and was unable to continue on its mission. In order to lighten its load and make it back to the base in England, they had to drop their four bombs, and all had landed in my neighborhood. Here comes the miracle. Out of the four bombs, three of them fell in harmless grass areas; only one fell on an apartment house and demolished it. All of us went to the bomb crater in the park the next day to look for pieces of the bomb. I found a few, and thought as I held them in my hand: "Gee, just think, just a few hours before, these pieces were still in England." That night, when it got dark, I was sure we would be bombed again. I couldn't sleep, and it was quite a while before I got a full night's sleep again.

The summer of 1941, was different from previous summer vacations, when I would go to the children's home in Zandvoort. This year no Jews were allowed to go to the beaches. My mother was desperate; what was she going to do with this wild one all summer? She contacted a nice

Jewish family in Heemstede, a small suburb of Haarlem, about 15 miles from Amsterdam. I was sent there to spend the summer. They had a daughter Hennie-Hettie, my age, whom I liked; she had dark hair with pigtails, and was sweet and soft, and we used to cuddle quite a bit, until one day her parents found out and threatened to take me to the police. I pleaded with them not to, and finally, after they made me promise never to do it again, (even though their daughter had started it) they gave me another chance.

I had a good time that summer, so my mother thought it would be a good idea if I stayed there; of course, I had nothing to say about it. I was enrolled in the local school, but not for long. About six weeks after school started, orders came that all Jews were to be evacuated to Amsterdam, and so I went home again. I visited my "adopted" family regularly in their apartment in Amsterdam, until one day I came and found the front door locked and sealed. They had been arrested the night before... I never saw them again.

The rest of 1942, things got progressively worse. The food rationing became smaller and smaller. All chickens were shipped off to Germany, also most of our cows. There was very little left for us. About once a week they would be very "generous" and release some milk for babies.

I always had an enterprising mind; and it was thought that someday "I would make it." As we lived on a canal, across the street from our house was a dock with space for boats to tie up. One of these boats carried milk in large cans from the farms into the city for distribution to the milkmen. As I watched this procedure, it dawned on me that when these large cans were emptied into smaller containers, there HAD to be some milk left in them. I waited until all the men were gone, went aboard the barge, lifted the cover of one of the cans, and sure enough, I was right. I ran home, got a glass and poured the little bit of milk left from each can into the glass, and drank it quickly, as it was a very warm day and the milk would soon turn sour.

Few people in those days had refrigerators, only the very rich ones, and so milk was delivered to the homes on a

34

daily basis. My mother always had to boil it first before she let me drink it. It wasn't until years later, after I had returned to the United States, that I had my first taste of ice-cold milk; it was delicious.

Back to the barge: I noticed that there was more milk left in the cans than I could consume. I ran home again, got some empty bottles, filled them, and sold them to our neighbors. I had to do this quickly for two reasons: the milk was not refrigerated, and I had to be careful not to get caught by the owner of the barge. One very hot day I must have delivered the milk to my "customers" a little late, and it turned sour. That was the end of my business, the end of my dreams of becoming the youngest dairy tycoon in Europe. Whenever sour milk becomes the "in" drink, I'll be back in business.

Then the nightmare really started. The "moffen" began to slowly but systematically go after the Jews. It began quite innocently. All the school children, Jews as well as Gentiles, were given a paper to take home for their father to fill out. Among many other questions was one in which we were asked how many Jewish grandparents we had. When I took this paper home, my Dad thought it was a "big joke," and wrote that I had FIVE Jewish grandparents. An announcement was made that according to their law passed in November 1935, you were Jewish if you had two or more Jewish grandparents.

Then the Germans ordered Mr. Ascher and Mr. Cohen, both famous diamond dealers, to head "De Joodse Raad" (The Jewish Advisory Bureau). After this office had been formed, Ascher and Cohen were notified by the Germans that it would be their job to see that each and every Dutch Jew would be deported to Poland within the next two months. The German term for this was: "Wir machen die Niederlanden Judenrein" (we will make the Netherlands clean of Jews). There were about 120,000 Jews living in Holland at that time, so they had some job ahead of them. They never finished it, but when it was all over, there were only 3000 left.

As soon as that news broke out, many Jewish families

went into hiding (underground), but this was not easy. You had to be lucky enough to know a non-Jewish family who was willing to risk their lives in hiding you, for God knows how long. It was common knowledge that if any people were caught hiding Jews, they would immediately be shot. In spite of this, many people took this chance. Another difficulty was food for the Jewish people in hiding. It had to be purchased on the black market. For this reason, many Jews went "underground" on farms throughout Holland. They were safer than the cities, and food was a little easier to get.

Some Jews with money, were "lucky" enough to buy citizenships to South American countries such as: Peru, Costa Rica, Equador, Paraguay, Nicaragua, Venezuela and Honduras. The consular representatives from these countries saw a great opportunity to make money, and sold passports to these unsuspecting people. The purchasers of these "citizenships" got a temporary sense of security; they thought they were "safe". In fact, they were, for a while. The Nazis were willing to accept these Jews as foreigners, and steps were taken to save them for future exchanges. But when the Germans made contact with these countries to verify the authenticity of their papers, the countries involved declined any knowledge of these people, and the result was that most of them were deported to the extermination camps.

Some of the Dutch Jews fared better and managed to escape Holland via the underground, and got to Switzerland and Spain, both neutral. Some even managed to get to Cuba and the United States. Others made contact with high-ranking Nazi officers and by bribing them with jewelry, money, paintings and other valuables (you couldn't take them with you anyway), made their get-away.

Unfortunately, my parents didn't think this was necessary, as we felt "protected" by my American citizenship. We had no place to go anyway; we didn't know of anyone who was willing to risk their lives for us, so we stayed put.

In May 1942, orders came that every Jew had to wear a large yellow Jewish star on all their clothes with the word

"JOOD" ("Jew" in Dutch). We were given one week to comply with this order. We not only had to pay for them, but had to give a textile ration coupon as well, which we could have used to buy a pair of socks. We needed them more than a star.

Although we were given several days to start wearing these "badges of honor," as they were called, most Jews wore them with pride the first day. The non-Jewish population showed their sentiments by wearing yellow flowers on their clothes. Underground posters were displayed throughout the city asking people, whenever they saw someone wearing a star, to show them the utmost respect.

What would have happened if we had to decide to go directly against orders and *not* wear the star? We all had neighbors who were Nazi sympathizers, and they would have been happy to report us to the authorities. They would have been rewarded for their "patriotism"; anyone who turned in a Jew was given 7½ guilders, about $2, for each.

After a few weeks, I received an official document stating that I did not have to wear the star, as I was an American. I have never been able to figure that one out; of course I was an American, but I was still Jewish. I found out later that this was all a part of their plan to treat foreigners with certain privileges to be used as tools later on. The first day I appeared on the street without my star, some of my neighbors who were Dutch Nazis, looked at me with hatred. They were just itching to pick up the phone to report me, but they knew it wouldn't do any good.

I suffered from mixed emotions during this time; I felt as if I had deserted my Jewish countrymen and family, and that I was "passing" as a non-Jew. On the other hand, there were many advantages, as I no longer had to abide by the many restrictions imposed upon the Jews, such as:

All Jews had to be in their homes by eight o'clock at night.

No Jew was allowed to ride on any public transportation, such as trains, streetcars, buses, or taxis.

Jews were no longer permitted to go to parks, zoos, theatres, beaches.

No Jews were allowed in any store except between the hours of three and five in the afternoon, as by that time about all the food, little as there was, was gone. It was very difficult to find a store we could go into, as most of the retailers had large signs in their windows: "NO JEWS ALLOWED."

Every Jew had to turn in his bicycle, as most Dutch people used them for transportation.

All Jewish businesses were taken over by the Germans, by putting in a Dutch Nazi in place of its rightful owner. These were called "Verwalters" (administrators), and many were people who had only been clerks in the business.

No Jew was allowed to socialize with non-Jews. This included schools, and all the Jewish kids were removed from their regular schools and put in "Jewish" schools in the ghetto. This was the only order I had to abide by.

One of the biggest advantages I had was that I could go shopping, in any store, at any time, and I did the shopping for our Jewish neighbors.

After the Jews had to wear the stars, there wasn't much for the children to do. There was a rich, elderly Jewish couple, Mijnheer en Mevrouw Druif, who lived in a beautiful house about a mile from mine. They loved children and opened their home to some of us, and we had an after-school club, complete with counselors. We sang songs, had arts and crafts, storytelling, and entertainment. I particularly remember a song and comedy team named: "Johnny en Jones," who were very popular at the time. They came to entertain us.

We had a play called: "De Koning Die Niet Lachen Kon" ("The King Who Couldn't Laugh"). Guess who got the leading role, the king?.... me, that's who. A cute girl, Ellie, was chosen to play the queen, and during rehearsals, as is common among us "showbiz" folks, we fell madly "in like" with each other. After rehearsals, I would walk her home, and it was decided she was to be my girlfriend. I was in sixth heaven (don't forget, Holland is just a small country, and we couldn't afford seven), and in spite of all the misery around us, my little world was a relatively happy one. But it wasn't to last.

One day as I was walking Ellie home, she told me she was going to tell me a big secret. She said: "Barry, what I am about to tell you, you must NEVER repeat to anyone, not even your father and mother, because my life would be in danger." I reassured her. She went on: "Tonight, around one in the morning, my parents, my brother Henri and I, are going away; we are going into hiding." I thought this was very exciting, but it seemed to be very depressing to her, when she continued, "But I will miss you so much, and what is going to happen to the play? Worst of all is that my father and mother are so afraid we are going to get caught, they decided to put me in one place, my brother in another, and my parents in still another. I have no idea where we are going, and of course I will never be able to write you, nor you to me, as I can never let you know where I am." It was a very sad goodbye, even for a couple of twelve-year-olds; as deep down inside, we both had the feeling we would probably never see each other again. I never stopped thinking about Ellie and would search for her wherever I went.

In the meantime, I was attending a special school for Jewish children only, with Jewish teachers. Every morning, the first thing we did was look around to see who was "missing," as this meant they had been arrested during the night and shipped off to the concentration camp in Holland, Westerbork. This was a transit camp, and from there they were sent to Poland. Our class decided to pull our resources together, and send packages to our classmates who had been shipped to Westerbork. Girls would make pancakes, others brought small packages of cheese, or salami, or tiny jars of jam.

By now the Germans had complete lists of all Jews living in Holland, all congregated in Amsterdam. It was easy for them to find these people at will, if they hadn't gone into hiding. First they sent notifications to every Jewish man between the ages of 16 and 35 in alphabetical order. They were told to report to a building in Amsterdam for a physical examination. If they qualified, they would never return home. They were sent to different concentration camps for slave labor, as only strong and healthy young men could produce hard labor.

39

I remember when my father was called to report for his physical. They gave him six days' notice. My father was not willing to go along and the only way to get out of it would be to be physically and/or mentally disqualified. Since he was mentally sound, the only thing left for him to do was to get physically disqualified. He went to our new family doctor, as Jews could no longer go to their regular doctor if he was a Gentile, to ask advice. He told my Dad to take two steam baths a day, as that would help him to lose weight. He did so, and along with that, he didn't eat for five whole days, except for some carrots and radishes. He walked ten to fifteen kilometers a day, running most of it, and did succeed in losing weight.

The day came for him to report for his examination. He left the house at eight o'clock in the morning, kissed my mother and me goodby, and we didn't know if we would ever see him again. My mother and I were very anxious, and when it got to be three in the afternoon, with no sign of him, we got worried. After hours of waiting nervously, it seemed like years; finally, at eight that night, we heard the front door open, and my Dad was home again. I am unable to describe the joy my mother and I felt when my father told us that he was... disqualified.

Aanmeldingsformulier voor één persoon,

die geheel of gedeeltelijk van joodschen bloede is (Verordening 6/1941)

Invullen met schrijfmachine of met inkt in blokletters

1.	Geslachtsnaam: (een vrouw vult hier alléén haar meisjesnaam in) Voornamen: (alle voluit)	
2.	Geboorteplaats: (gemeente) Datum van geboorte: (dag, maand en jaar)	
3.	Woon- of verblijfplaats: Straat en huisnummer: Laatste woonplaats in het Groot-Duitsche Rijk (met inbegrip van het Protectoraat Bohemen en Moravië) of van het Gouvernement-Generaal voor het bezette Poolsche gebied: (invullen voor hen, die na 30 Januari 1933 in Nederland geïmmigreerd zijn)	
4.	Nationaliteit: en Eventueele vroegere nationaliteiten:	
5.	Kerkelijke gezindte:	
6.	Beroep of werkzaamheid: (duidelijk omschrijven)	
7.	Ongehuwd, gehuwd, weduwnaar, weduwe of gescheiden van echt: (naam en voornamen van echtgenoot(e) of gewezen echtgenoot(e) voluit)	gehuwd met: weduwnaar van: weduwe gescheiden van:
8.	De onder 1 vermelde persoon: a. behoorde op 9 Mei 1940 tot de joodsch-kerkelijke gemeente b. is na dien datum daarin opgenomen c. was op 9 Mei 1940 met een jood gehuwd d. is na dien datum met een jood in het huwelijk	ja/neen ja/neen ja/neen ja/neen
9.	Hoeveel joodsche grootouders in den zin van artikel 2 der verordening (zie keerzijde): (invullen in letters)	
10.	Opmerkingen	

Niet zelf invullen

Ingekomen d.d.

ƒ 1,— { voldaan / niet voldaan

Vermindering   Reden: <br> tot een bedrag van ƒ
 Vrijstelling:

Vergeleken met en aanduiding geplaatst op:
 Persoonskaart
 Verblijfregister
 Sign. aangebracht
 Bew. v. aanmelding afgegeven d.d.

Verzonden aan } Hoofd R. Insp. { d. d.
 Ontvangen door } Bevolk. reg. { d. d.

Par. ambt.

Ondergeteekende verklaart het vorenstaande naar waarheid te hebben ingevuld.

Gemeente

1941

(handteekening aanmeldingsplichtige)

Uitgegeven met toestemming van het hoofd der Rijksinspectie van de bevolkingsregisters beschikking dd. 31 Januari 1941 nr. 5

"9. How many Jewish grandparents?"

Voor Joden verboden

DE PROCUREUR-GENERAAL
FUNG. GEWESTELIJK DIRECTEUR VAN POLITIE

FEITSMA

"FOR JEWS PROHIBITED"

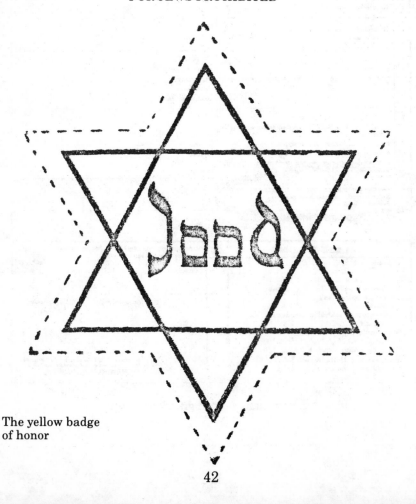

The yellow badge
of honor

42

Amsterdam, 13.Juli 1942
Heerengracht 545.

Herrn und Frau A.B. Spanjaar
und Kind,

Amstelkade 10 II,
A M S T E R D A M Z.

Austausch U.S.A.

Ich beehre mich Ihnen zur Kenntnis zu bringen, dass, laut einem soeben eingegangenen Bericht d. Schutzmachtangelegenheiten der Schweizerischen Gesandtschaft in Berlin, Ihre Teilnahme an einem allfälligen Austauschtransport nch den U.S.A. von den zuständigen amerikanischen Behörden genehmig worden ist.

Hochachtend,

DER VERWESER DES
SCHWEIZERISCHEN KONSULATS:

Our notification from the Swiss Consul (Walter Spycher) that we have been approved by Berlin for a possible exchange to the U.S.A.

43

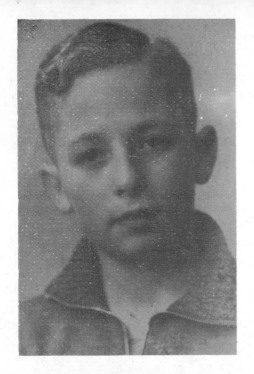

My Bar Mitzvah picture

The little synagogue on the Lekstraat where
I was Bar Mitzvah on July 26, 1942.

My Bar Mitzvah rings - first and last look.

Der Befehlshaber
der Sicherheitspolizei und des SD
für die besetzten niederl.Gebiete
Lager Westerbork

Lager Westerbork,d. 17.August 194 2 ..

Entlassungsschein.

Der Jude ~~die~~~~~~~~~~~ Alfred Bernard S p a n j a a r d

geb.am: 28.7.03   in: Amsterdam

ist am: 17.August 1942   entlassen.

Gründe: lt.Gesuch des Schweizerischen Konsulates (Sohn amerik.

             Staatsbürger)

Er/~~Sie~~ ist verpflichtet, sich unverzüglich bei der Zentralstelle für
jüdische Auswanderung, Amsterdam-Zuid, Adema van Scheltemaplein 1, zu
melden und diesen Entlassungsschein vorzulegen. Reisegenehmigung zur
Fahrt nach Amsterdam ist ~~erteilt~~ ...

Hat die Erlaubnis ~~sich~~
nach 8 Uhr abends ~~~~
auf der Strasse zu bewegen.

[signature]

. Sturmbannführer und
Regierungsrat

"The Jew Alfred Bernard Spanjaard......
is released from Camp Westerbork....by
request of Swiss Consul, son American
citizen."

46

V. LITTLE AMERICAN POWER

At this point the relationship between my father and mother improved. They seemed to grow closer, and it made for a harmonious atmosphere in the house, which made me happy.

Because the "moffen" were never satisfied with the amount of young Jewish men they were able to deport, they got another brainstorm. I would wake up many times from the noise made by heavy trucks, and from my window could see the whole neighborhood being surrounded by the Grune Polizei. They would go from house to house, searching for Jews, and bring them down, at gunpoint, to their trucks. They took babies, pregnant women, sick or old people; all had to come along, with no special consideration, to be brought to the trains and sent to Westerbork. Whenever they came to our house, they let us stay because of my American papers.

The Jewish religion has a very nice tradition dating back thousands of years, that when a boy becomes thirteen years old, he will be "Bar Mitzvah." In olden days a Jewish boy would get his education until he was thirteen years old, and at that time he was considered to be a man. It is a strong tradition and is probably the most important day in his life; even bigger than his marriage, because he shares that day with another person, his bride. This is strictly for HIM. Even though my parents were not very religious, they still wanted me to become Bar Mitzvah'd. This meant several years of studying Hebrew and Judaism, and on the big day, be called up to the pulpit in a synagogue to recite a special portion of the Torah, the Jewish scrolls of learning. The boy's father is also called up and recites the ancient prayer: "Blessed be He who releases me from the responsibility of this child."

My Bar Mitzvah was to be, according to the Jewish calendar, July 26th, 1942. We were living in a Nazi-occupied country, where Jewish services were no longer permitted. But where there's a will, there's a way, and we found it. I studied for this occasion, as I had to know Jewish history, prayers, customs, and, hardest of all, Hebrew, which I found very difficult. Somehow, my parents found a rabbi (teacher) who was willing to take a chance, and he secretly came to our house twice a week to prepare me for my Bar Mitzvah. Very reluctantly, as most boys are, I studied with him for a year.

Now came the big problem; how to conduct services in a synagogue without arousing suspicion? Going as a group would be dangerous, as it would be very tempting for the Germans to find many Jews together in one place.

The house of worship, chosen for the ceremony of "my becoming a man" was the "sjoel" in the Lekstraat, about two miles from my house. My parents, my grandmother, a few close friends (most had been deported by that time) and I walked to the synagogue, but NOT together. We left the house, one at a time, at five minute intervals. In those days you couldn't trust anyone, not even your friends or neighbors, and you never knew who would turn you in.

After the short and secret ceremony, we returned to my house, the same way we had come, one by one. We had a small reception, my mother served some tea and cookies she had somehow managed to get.

One of the highlights of the day was yet to come. Dad called me into the bedroom and showed me a collection of beautiful rings which had been left for me by his father. I had never seen them before, nor knew of their existence, so it came as a big surprise. But again, we had to be very careful. If someone knew, and told the Germans, they would have been taken away. Dad very carefully took out a little box, told me what he was going to show me, and said for me never to tell anyone about this. I would be allowed to look at them for a few minutes, and then they would have to be put back in a secret hiding place. When I opened the box, I saw six beautiful gold rings with large precious stones; red, white, yellow, green and blue. I was very impressed; but then, as I had been told, they were taken away for after the war. They were then returned to their "secret" hiding place. It was so safe and secret that I never saw them again.

This happened with other valuables my Dad hid. During the first few years of the war my father, as well as many other people, made more money than he had ever made before. Money didn't have much value and losing more every day, but art, diamonds, rare coins and books, were good investments. Many people invested in these collections, and as my Dad was in this business, he made good commissions. He too wanted to invest some of his earnings, and started a beautiful collection of rare old books as well as first editions, and the entire wall of our living room was filled with them. He had special book shelves built for these as well as the many books he still had from his youth. These too disappeared.

He also invested in old gold coins (goude tientjes) and carefully put them in a large jar. He and one of our neighbors, who was not Jewish, went and buried this treasure somewhere in Amsterdam.

Eleven days after my Bar mitzvah, August 6th, 1942, was "Black Thursday." It was a beautiful day during our summer vacation from school, but there wasn't much to do because of all the restrictions. I left the house at about nine o'clock that morning and walked a few blocks until I came to a bridge called De Berlage Brug, named for a famous Dutch architect. This bridge is over the Amstel river, which separates Amsterdam East from Amsterdam South, where I lived. On the bridge were a squad of German policemen, who were stopping everyone who wanted to cross in either direction. The "gentlemen" were having another one of their "razzias" (roundups). Before this day was over they picked up over 2000 Jews, more than ever before, and it became known as "Black Thursday." They did their usual house-to-house search, and anyone wearing a Jewish star was put in large trucks and taken away. As soon as I understood what was happening, I ran home to tell my parents about it, but there was nothing they could do. My mother assured me: "Don't worry, Barry, with your American birth certificate, we are safe."

In spite of this calming statement, I still had the feeling that something was going to happen. We could see them coming closer and closer to *our* house. Defenseless men, women and children were being pushed into big heavy trucks; a terrible sight. I was too upset to stay home, so I went downstairs and watched in the street. I wasn't wearing the yellow star, so I knew they wouldn't bother me. By this time, the Grune Polizei was only one house away from mine. After about ten minutes, I saw six people taken from their home at gunpoint and shoved into a big, heavy, smelly truck.

One of them was my friend Felix, whom I had grown up with, and spent many hours of my life. He looked terrified, and as he passed me we looked into each others eyes. He looked as though to say: "Help me, help me!" But I had to stand there, helpless, there was nothing I could do for him. It was like watching one of your best friends drowning, and all you do is stand there doing nothing.

After they had been taken away, four husky German policemen, armed with loaded rifles and bayonets, approached the steps of our house. For the first time in my life, I had the feeling I was going to faint. Again, I had to wait about ten minutes, but it seemed more like years. They were searching the whole building. Finally, I saw my father and mother come down with their hands above their heads. The policemen didn't know I was their son, for two reasons: I wasn't wearing a star. Secondly, my parents, of course, had not told them they had a son, with the hope of saving me from their clutches. As they reached the street, I walked up to them; perhaps I could do something for them, or at least say goodbye. As far as I knew at that moment, it would be the last time I would ever see them. As I approached my helpless father and mother, a German jumped toward me and yelled: "Gehen sie wag!" (go away) At that moment I could have murdered him. As he pushed me away with his big rough hands, I heard the other guard say to my parents; "Wenn Sie ruhe, ich schiesse" (If you move, I'll shoot). They were shoved into a big truck and driven away.

Here I was, my father and mother gone... I was now by myself, a 12 year old boy. I didn't know what to do next. A few minutes before, my Dad had managed to whisper to me: "Don't worry, Barry, everything will be all right." That was some joke, how COULD everything be all right? For a few minutes I just stood there, not knowing what to do. Some neighbors passed, giving me sympathetic looks or smiles, as if they were trying to say that they were sorry, but were helpless to do anything about it.

Then, I got a bright idea... I could make an important phone call. We had a phone in the house, but for some reason or other, I was scared to go up there. So I ran to the corner grocery store, as I knew they had a phone, and called the Swiss Consul. During the war, the American consul had left Holland and closed up the embassy, and the Swiss consul was now representing him. He was the only one left who might be able to help me get my father and mother back. I told him what had happened, and he said he would do everything in his power for me, and I should phone him back later.

Usually the "captured" Jews were taken to "De Hollandsche Schouwburg," an old, large theatre in the middle of the Jewish ghetto.

That afternoon, I phoned the consul again. Maybe he would have some good news for me.... but he didn't. All he was able to tell me was that he was working hard for me and that he had gone, personally, to the Grüne Polizei headquarters in Amsterdam and told them that the parents of a minor American citizen had been taken to the Schouwburg. Again he told me to phone him back, perhaps he would have some better news. I waited another two hours, when he told me he had permission from the Grune Polizei headquarters to go to the Schouwburg and have my parents released. He went there personally to tell the guards to let my parents go home. They even allowed him to go on stage and announce their names. Five times he had called out: "Mr. and Mrs. Spanjaard may leave now and return to their home!" But there was no answer from the imprisoned audience... my parents were not there!

That was all the news the consul had for me. I felt hopeless and alone, and pictured my parents already on their way to some horrible concentration camp. By this time it was getting dark and I began to feel worse by the minute. There I was, all alone, no father, no mother, in this big house without any hope for the future. How was I going to feed myself, how was I going to pay the rent, what was to become of me? All these thoughts were running through my mind. I didn't go to bed, as I wouldn't have been able to sleep anyway... Suddenly, I heard our front door open... it was my mother! I was so glad to see her—I cried from joy. She looked very tired, but I had about 1001 questions to ask her. Where had they brought them? Where was my father? Why did they let her go? But I could see clearly by the expression on her face that she was ill. In spite of the way she was feeling, she sat down and tried to explain the whole situation to me.

They had been taken to a school instead, and *not* the theatre, and were kept there to be transported later to Westerbork—About four o'clock that afternoon she had become very ill, and asked one of the guards if it would be possible to see a doctor. He sent her upstairs to see the German S.S. doctor, where they made her wait five hours, standing all the time, before she was allowed to enter his office. Finally, a guard told her that the doctor would see her. He gave her a quick examination, realized that she was indeed very ill, and wrote out a pass for her to return home. He also gave her a permit allowing her to walk on the street after the Jewish curfew of 8 p.m., so she wouldn't be arrested. I never could figure out how she managed to persuade an S.S. man to release her. I had never heard of anyone being released just because they were sick. Her talent for dramatics had paid off.

When my mother asked the doctor if my Dad could go with her, he gave her a sarcastic smile, as only Germans did so well. She had to walk about four miles, because she was not allowed to use public transportation. When she finally arrived home, she was exhausted. Things began to get a little clearer to me; now I knew why there had been no answer in the Schouwburg that afternoon... my parents had never been there at all. About the only thing left for us to do that night was to go to bed and try to sleep, but neither of us were able to. I could imagine my Daddy behind barbed wire in one of those camps we had heard so much about. I could see him being beaten by one of those young S.S. guards. I actually had nightmares about it, and was happy to see the daylight break through the quiet night.

That day was rough for my mother and me, not to mention my Dad, who was locked up. Somehow we had to get him from lion's mouth. But how to go about it? My mother, who felt a little better in the morning, went immediately to the Swiss consul's office. I jumped on my dad's bicycle and went to "De Joodse Raad" (a council organized for the benefit of the Dutch Jews), but I couldn't find any help there. I realized that I couldn't sit and let them take my father to a concentration camp. I didn't care what would happen to me, I just had to keep on trying. Again I jumped on my bicycle and rode to the school on the Adema van Scheltemaplein, in Amsterdam, which had become the headquarters for the Grüne Polizei.

Now I knew that my father, as well as all those other people who had been picked up the day before was being held there. I wasn't afraid; I wasn't wearing a yellow Jewish star, so none of the guards there would know I was Jewish. After a ten minute ride, I arrived at the school, put my bike against one of the walls. The entire place was surrounded by the Grune Polizei with machine guns. I walked around the school, which was a whole block, carefully observing everything, trying to find a spot where perhaps I could climb over a wall, or go under a fence. But there was absolutely no way of sneaking in. I walked up to one of the guards and started to talk to him, not realizing that he couldn't understand my Dutch. Soon a Dutch policeman came to my rescue, and translated for me.

I told him a story that one of my neighbors was there, and I had to bring him an important message from his wife...I was smart enough not to tell him that it was my own father, because I was sure he would never let me in. After he thought for a few seconds, to my great surprise he gave me permission to go and see my "neighbor." He told me I had twenty minutes, and I needed every second of that, with hundreds of people it might take me twenty minutes just to find my Dad. For the first time I thought I had actually met up with a decent German. I didn't let him say it a second time! I practically flew inside. After I looked around the crowd, I located my father.

It was horrible for me to see Dad in this situation, and the first few minutes I couldn't get a word out of my mouth, I was too choked up. Finally, we both managed a conversation. My father was sure he was going to be sent away, and concerned that he didn't have any baggage. They hadn't given him any time to take anything with him, not even an extra pair of socks. He asked me if I could try to bring him his overcoat, toilet articles, and a couple of other small items, which at the time seemed so important to him. I told him I would go home immediately, though I did not know how I could manage to get these things to him. I went home, gathered what my Dad had asked for, packed them in a suitcase, and left the house. I didn't see my mother, as she had been gone since early morning trying desperately to get my Dad freed.

Well, here I was again—me on the outside, trying to get in—and all those poor people on the inside, trying to get out, behind those thick, high, grey walls, being held against their will. They hadn't done anything wrong. The only thing they were "guilty" of was that they happened to be born Jewish. Now I had to think up another story, so the guard would let me in again. How I managed it I really don't know, but I found myself inside again a few minutes later talking to my Dad. I gave him his overcoat and the suitcase filled with the things he had asked for, and he was very thankful. He asked me: "How is your mother feeling, and how is she taking all this?" I told him: "Mommy is feeling better and is trying everything to get you out of all this." He was very happy to hear that. I told him: "I am going home now to see if there is anything new, and pack some more things for you and try to get in to see you again later, but I can't promise that I can."

When I came home, my mother had returned. She told me that the consul was doing everything he could for us. I believed my mother, but didn't have much hope that anything could be done. Then bad news reached us; everyone being held at that school was to be transported to Westerbork. We felt completely helpless. My mother was very worried. As an adult, she was more aware of what was happening and was going to happen than I, as a child. We started packing some more things for my father in a couple of dufflebags. Some sympathetic neighbors came over to help us, and also brought some cigarettes, cigars, cheese, jam, and other foods, a great sacrifice to them. That's the way Dutch people are. They tried to cheer us up, but that was impossible.

By the time we had everything packed, it was eight o'clock at night and we had to hurry. It was too much baggage for me to carry by myself, so one of our neighbors was nice enough to help me by going along on his bicycle, carrying some of the bags. On the way back to the school, we were stopped several times by the police who wanted to know where we were going with all that baggage. We told them that we were helping somebody move to another apartment. I was learning to lie quite well, but it was a matter of necessity. We finally reached the schoolhouse, where others were trying to get in for a last chance to see their relatives and loved ones, most of them realizing that this would probably be the last time. They were wearing the Jewish star, and weren't allowed in, were chased away, and told if they wouldn't leave right away, they too would be arrested.

This time I was very doubtful that I would be let in again. As I was walking around that school trying desperately to get inside, I thought, who was I trying to see? Who was preventing me from doing so? The *criminals* were on the outside, guarding the *innocent* people on the inside. The Nazis knew of no courts, no justice. They sentenced these people who were waiting there, unable to do anything until it was decided to kill them. The unfairness of it all really hit me.

I counted twenty-five armed guards around the high school walls. I went to every single one to see if HE would let me in, with no luck. Then I saw that I had skipped just one guard, at the main entrance. I walked up to him like a man, but in front of this 6 footer, I felt like a mouse. While I was trying to explain to him that my father was behind those walls, I started to cry. To my great surprise, he seemed to care. He suddenly stepped in front of me, and gave me a shove into the hallway. My father had already spotted me talking to this guard, and was waiting.

Those few precious moments with him were heartbreaking for both of us. Without saying it, we both realized the seriousness of the situation, and knew that there was a good possibility we would never see each other again. I was crying, and couldn't talk, so my Dad tried to console me, but there wasn't much he could say to make me feel better. He tried to take my mind off the situation by telling me that I was now the "man" of the house and it was my job to take care of my mother. He gave me his watch, the house-key and a few other personal things. Then an announcement was made for the prisoners to get ready, as they were leaving for the transport in a few minutes. Then I had to leave.

I went home and had to tell my mother that he was gone...The only thing she could manage to say, through her tears was: "Maybe God will help us, let's pray for his return." It seems that when we are in need of something, or are hungry or sick, we turn to God. Why don't we always believe in Him?

The next day came, without us having slept the night before. We were both exhausted and hungry, as we had given most of our food to my Dad. We had to wait until the next ration coupons were issued before we could buy more.

Then more bad news reached us: rumors were going around that on the next day, Tuesday, a transport of 5,000 Dutch Jews would be sent to Poland.

We were unaware exactly what this meant. We did know that these concentration camps were horrible places to be, but we did NOT know that some of these camps were for the sole purpose of exterminating people. We realized that slave labor was performed, but always lived in the hope that the war would someday be over, and all of them would come home.

Something had to be done for my father; we just couldn't let him go without trying everything that was humanly possible.

For a couple of years we had a Christian cleaning lady come to our house twice a week to help my mother with the housework. When she arrived that day and heard about what had happened to my father, she became very upset. She told us: "I went to school with Mussert, and I am going to his headquarters in The Hague to talk to him and ask him to send Mr. Spanjaard home." (The Mussert she referred to was the head of the N.S.B.—the Dutch Nazi Party).

She came back the next day after seeing Mussert, and he had told her, after doing some checking, that my father would be released. But after all the promises that had been made to us by the Swiss consul, and now this Mussert, we had become very doubtful.

The next day my grandmother came to visit us. When she heard the news, she fainted. Within a few minutes the doorbell rang. It was a man bringing us a telegram, and we literally tore it open. In the excitement my mother almost forgot to tip the delivery man. It was from my father from Westerbork, and it read: "Was pulled out of the train stop am temporarily held back stop love Fred stop" The train he referred to was the dreaded transport to Auschwitz. I can't describe our joy. At least he was saved from this transport, but we all knew there would be another one next week; as they had them every Tuesday morning. My grandmother was on the bed and still in a daze. We tried to tell her the good news we had just received.

About two hours later, the regular mail came with a long letter from Dad. It had been smuggled out of Westerbork, and was written on toilet paper. The most important part of the letter was, that the reason he had been pulled off the train was that he was the father of a dependent American-born child. The consul had arranged this for us. At that point I was glad that I had remained in Holland, and that my Mother had gone through the trouble of registering me every two years as an American. If this had not been done, my father would have been on his way to Auschwitz. I knew then I had made the right decision to stay in Holland.

The next day we received another letter from Dad, and this time it contained even better news...he was coming home! He wrote us that he didn't know exactly when it would be, so we just had to wait again. On the next day another telegram came. "WILL BE HOME WEDNESDAY ONE PM STOP" It was ten o'clock in the morning, so we had about three hours to do things to prepare for his homecoming. We decorated the whole house. I didn't know how, but the news went around the neighborhood like wildfire. Everyone was very happy that he was coming home; it was really the first time that anyone had *ever* heard of someone being released from a concentration camp, and they came to congratulate us. Because we were so busy, the time had flown, and it was now 12:30.

We looked around the house to check if everything was right, and it was just perfect. I just couldn't hold back any longer, I had to go downstairs to meet my father. I waited about twenty minutes, and there he came walking towards me. At first I didn't recognize him, as he had a beard and was very thin, and looked tired as he carried two duffel-bags on his shoulders. He was home again!!

One of the first things he did was to show us the official document he had been given by the S.S. Commandant of Westerbork, releasing him.

We had a small party, and friends brought us useful things, eggs, butter, coffee beans, cheese as well as their good wishes. That was indeed an unforgettable day. It was just wonderful to have him home again, and we settled down to a somewhat normal life again. His release gave us a sense of security; we figured as long as my father had been relesed from the camp, it meant that the Germans had given their official recognition of my American citizenship, so we no longer had "anything to fear." We were safe...

The street where we lived, Amstelkade 10 (apartment circled) from 1932 until our arrest.

VI. EXPENSIVE PATRIOTISM

Though we felt safe, it was a completely different story for other Jews in Amsterdam. A family, good friends of ours, Mr. and Mrs. A., lived about three blocks from us. They were nice people and we used to visit them often, and I enjoyed playing with their two sons, Max and Simon. Max was 18, and Simon was my age, 13. One day two Gestapo (GEheime STAats POlizei—Secret State Police) paid a "visit" to the A. family. They came to get their older son, Max. When they were told that he wasn't home, they were not satisfied. They noticed the younger brother playing in his room and said they would take him and keep him until the older boy turned himself in.

The parents didn't know what to do—they were going crazy with worry and fear. Should they turn in their older son to the Gestapo in order to get the younger one back? Mrs. A. made the decision: Since they could not trust the Gestapo, as they were afraid that they would keep *both* their sons, they decided to save the older boy, by not turning him in. Ten o'clock that night, Mr. and Mrs. A. received a telegram; "Your son has been killed trying to escape."

I will always remember October 19th, 1942, when the "brave" members of the Grüne Polizei decided to raid the home for the blind, on the Amsteldijk. These people worked making rugs, brushes and other household items, which were then sold so they could support themselves and not be a burden on the State. They were all Jews in their fifties

61

and sixties. It was a great opportunity for the Nazis to gather up about 100 helpless people, all at once. I was passing by the home when this "razzia" took place. It was a pitiful sight, watching these big men shoving poor, totally defenseless people into those trucks. No one ever heard from them again.

One afternoon on my way to visit my grandmother who was living in the Jewish ghetto, I passed a maternity hospital, and witnessed another one of their deeds. They were arresting all the women in the building, including the ones who were about to give birth and those who had just given birth. They threw these women and babies into their waiting trucks. As the trucks pulled away, I saw blood dripping from them.

Then the Germans took all the telephones and radios away. They had found out about the secret radio broadcasts every night from England, called "Radio Oranje," named after the Dutch royal family of Oranje. From these broadcasts we got some facts as to what was going on in the world. The Germans would only give THEIR version of the news. My parents looked forward to these newscasts every night. They also contained secret messages for the resistance. Then the "moffen" found out, and a notice was put out that if anyone was caught listening to these broadcasts they would be jailed immediately. However, the people ignored these orders, so the radios were taken away. They treated us like children. When you ask a child to stop playing with something, and he doesn't, you take it away from him.

They came in the middle of the night to make sure you were home. If you were, and Jewish, they would just take you with them, never to be returned. This happened to us, not once or twice, but *thirteen* times. But thirteen times they left us at home, because my parents would show them my American registration papers.

The first time they came was about three o'clock in the morning, and it took my parents a few minutes to get to the door. They didn't like that and told my parents that when they came the next time, if the door wasn't opened immediately, they would shoot my father. We knew they meant business, as we had heard several cases where this happened. So, one night my mother would stay up, and the next night my father; so at least one of them would be ready at all times to open the door as soon as the doorbell rang.

While on some errands for my mother, I ran into Sam, my friend, with his father, mother and little sister. They had just returned from the doctor and were on their way home. Suddenly, out of nowhere, a car drove up, pulled over to the sidewalk, and stopped. Two civilians came out. They saw that my friend and his family were wearing the Jewish star, and told them that they would have to come along with them. We all knew what that meant...they would not be coming back. Just before getting into the car, Mr. L. reached in his pocket and took out some keys and threw them to me and said: "Please, Barry, if you have a chance, go to our house, pack a few suitcases with some essentials for us, find out where they took us, and bring the suitcases to us so we have something to wear. Please, Barry, try..." And with that they were driven off. So quick..., one minute I was standing talking to my friends and the next minute they were gone.

When I went home and told my mother what happened, she suggested that I try to do what they asked me. I told her I probably would be home late, as I didn't know how long it would take me. At least I didn't have to worry about the 8 o'clock curfew.

I went to their house, carefully looked around all the drawers and closets for clothes, and tried to find some food I could take to them. I packed three suitcases, as I couldn't carry anymore by myself.

Somehow I managed to drag these a few blocks where I took the streetcar to the Hollandsche Schouwburg. When I got there, I found a lot of confusion, but with some difficulty managed to get to the administration desk. I asked permission to see the family L. A woman looked on several lists she had in front of her, and told me that she was sorry, but there was no such family there. I told her what had happened, and she said that there were a few people who had been arrested that day who had been taken straight to the train that was leaving for Westerbork in an hour.

First, I had to find out where this train was and how to get there. After taking two more streetcars, I finally got to the train, except that I had to walk about two miles to get there. Totally exhausted, I reached it, loaded with people, about a thousand men, women and children, ready to be taken to a concentration camp. I had to find four people out of this mass. I took a chance, and put the suitcases down as I couldn't carry them any longer. Slowly, I walked along the train, looking carefully into each compartment, and sure enough...I found them. I told them I had the suitcases and it would just be a few minutes to go get them. They told me to hurry, as they were about to leave. I ran as fast as I could, picked up the suitcases and tried to run to get back to my friend's compartment. They opened the door, and I handed them the suitcases, just as the train started to pull out of the station. Then I had to say goodbye to my buddy, a boy I had known almost all my life, had run around with, had been in the same class with for several years, had chased girls with. More than likely I would never see him again. His parents yelled to me from the open window that they were very grateful I had done this for them. The only thing that helped me at this time was that I had been able to do something for these sad people. Sam, his father, mother, sister, never returned....

I started to cry like a baby. Except for a few "Joodse Raad" officials, I was all alone on the big station platform. I cried all the way back to the streetcar, as I watched the train pull out of the station until it disappeared in the distance.

I cried and cried, unashamedly; I didn't care who saw me. I thought about this incident many times, and I often wondered why I cried then, and why, when it finally happened to ME just a few months later... I didn't cry at all...

Our "lords and masters" liked to date pretty Dutch girls, but the girls who went out with them were much resented

64

by the Dutch people. Not all the girls did so willingly.

Nannie, who I used to play with, was raped at the point of a gun by a German soldier, and became pregnant. She was later sent to the notorious Auschwitz concentration camp in Poland, where the baby was born, but killed instantly. She never left the camp alive...

I had always been proud of my city, Amsterdam and particularly my own neighborhood, but it was no longer a pleasant experience to take a walk through the streets in my area. In almost every business establishment I passed, were signs saying: "VOOR JODEN VERBODEN" (For Jews prohibited), not only in stores, but bars, nightclubs, restaurants, theatres, even public parks. We weren't even allowed to sit on benches anymore. These signs made us feel degraded and depressed. Most Dutch people didn't want those signs, but the Germans made this an official order; otherwise, they would close their businesses.

The world famous Rijksmuseum is located in the heart of Amsterdam, and houses some of the greatest masterpieces by such artists as: Rembrandt, Van Gogh, Vermeer and Frans Hals. My father and I had gone there often on Saturday afternoons, because we both enjoyed beautiful paintings. Now, of course, we could not. We were not the only ones who appreciated fine art, the Germans did too, and got these masterpieces at a bargain; in fact, without paying for them...they would take them and ship them off to the High Command in Germany. Fortunately, they didn't get them all. The Dutch had been smart enough to take some of the priceless pieces and hide them in caves in Holland. Those that were not hidden were found after the war in the homes of Hitler, Goering and Goebbels, and were returned to their rightful place, for people from all over the world to enjoy and appreciate.

Life for everyone in Holland got worse. We had brutal winters, there was no coal for heating, food got more scarce, and we lived constantly in fear of being bombed. On top of that, it was even worse for the Jews who lived from day to day worrying about being arrested and shipped off to a concentration camp. Every night as I went to sleep, I thanked God for letting us stay at home for another day.

Although we were not starving, we constantly were hungry. This does odd things to people; they become nervous, irritable, short-tempered and selfish. At four o'clock in the morning, they would start lining up in front of the bakeries, even though they didn't open until two in the afternoon; in the hope of buying a single loaf of bread. Most of the time they were turned down.

One could buy almost everything through the black market. Enormous prices were paid, and farmers who had been poor before the war, became very rich, selling such items as potatoes, cheese, butter, milk and meat. When people ran out of money, they would use jewelry, diamonds and coin collections as payment on the black market.

A story making the rounds in those days was about a Jewish farmer who had been sent to a camp. His wife wrote him a letter, telling him that she didn't know what to do about the potato fields, as they were ready to be plowed; and with him in the camp, there was no one left to do the job. Her husband wrote back telling her not to worry about it, as he had hidden diamonds in the fields. The Germans censored this letter, and immediately sent a crew to the farm to dig up the diamonds. They, of course, found nothing, but in the meantime, they had done a fine job plowing up her crop.

One day, a tiny light broke through for us, at least it seemed that way. We received a letter from the Swiss consul, asking us to come to his office as soon as possible. As we thought it must be something important, we left immediately. The consul told us: "We have received permission from the German authorities to start preparing a list of people with American papers who might be considered for an "Austausch" (exchange). The Americans have come to an agreement with the Germans to return five German nationals or prisoners of war, for each American citizen they release. Do you wish to be considered for this?" There we were, with another invitation to go to America, but this time it was different from the ones I had received during the five war days...this time my parents were allowed to go with me. As my Dad was not at this meeting because he was working, the consul said: "Why don't you go home and talk it over with your husband, and you can let me know in the next few days, at which time you can come back to my office, as you will have to sign some papers."

My mother and I were thrilled at the prospect of going back to the United States, but when we got home my father shocked us when he said that he did not want to go. We couldn't believe our ears when we heard this, but he had his reasons. First, he was extremely patriotic towards Holland, as he had a good life there. Secondly, he did not want to abandon his mother. And last, but not least, he did not want to "run away like a coward," and said that he would never be able to ever look another Dutchman in the eye. Besides that, hadn't the Germans already released him from Westerbork? He said we would not be bothered again.

Both my mother and I wanted to go back to America, as we always had, even before the war; especially now, when the world around us was falling apart. All hell broke loose in our house; my father and mother must have argued for hours. My mother with her persuasive manner, with me in her corner for once, finally managed to talk my father into agreeing to come with us to the consul the next day to sign the necessary papers. We phoned the consul and told him of "our" decision and he told us that we should have pictures taken for our passports.

The next day we went to the consul's office, gave him the pictures, signed some papers, and he told us to be prepared to leave without much notice. He mailed us an official document regarding this.

We were ready all right, and for a long time, but nothing came of it until much later...too much later.

There was a big bank in Amsterdam owned by two Jewish men, Lippmann & Rosenthal. The Germans took it over and confiscated all the money that had been deposited into Jewish accounts. Furthermore, they used this bank to get other possessions owned by Dutch Jews, such as jewelry, stocks, bonds, and insurance policies. As my father was also an insurance broker, we had insurance for everything since 1932. My father was forced to turn in all those policies to Lippman & Rosenthal, and that was the end of that. The winters were particularly unpleasant, because the Germans had taken all the coal out of our coalmines and shipped it off to Germany. So we started to burn wood, which also became very scarce. Shoes were just impossible to get, so we started to wear the world famous wooden shoes (klompen). At first this was difficult and painful, but once we got used to them, they were warm, dry and comfortable.

The few Jewish people that were left in Holland by this time knew that any day might be the end of their freedom. So they started to hide valuable things, they had managed not to turn in, with Christian friends, in the hope of recovering them after the war. Few ever came back to reclaim their possessions.

Each day we would notice more empty houses. That was the sign that the night before, the inhabitants had been arrested. People had begun to get so cold and hungry that they started to steal. As soon as Jews had been dragged from their homes, the plunderers would attack the house like vultures. They would break the windows, enter the house and take everything that was of any value, even the wood from the window-sills to be used as fuel. People get that way out of desperation.

The Germans put a stop to this by sealing off the houses as soon as the people had been arrested. Anyone entering these homes would immediately be shot on the spot; after all, the Nazis had their own plans for these possessions... to ship them to Germany. They contracted with a large Amsterdam moving company, Puls, to go into those homes the next day, empty them, and take the goods to Germany. This became known as: "Pulsen."

There was a strong and effective underground as well as a resistance movement in Holland. To the best of my knowledge, the difference between the two was; the underground would help Jews over the border, print phony identity papers; and, last but not least, help Jews go into hiding and protect them after they got there. The resistance movement, on the other hand, would do sabotage, and relay military information to the Allies in England. They regularly blew up radio stations, trains, and attacked and killed many German soldiers whose bodies would usually end up in one of our many canals. This only added to the pollution. Official German military cars were pushed into those canals as well.

Because of all this resistance and sabotage, the Nazis created an organization called the W.A. (Weer Afdeling), to fight the resistance and arrest its participants. It consisted of Dutchmen who were members in good standing of the Nazi Party, and was headed by Hendrik Koot, but he didn't have that pleasure for long. He was killed by the very people he was supposed to arrest, soon after he accepted his new office.

The "moffen" had to blame this act on someone, so naturally the Jews were *again* the "chosen people." They posted bulletins all over Amsterdam giving the guilty men three days to surrender, or strict measures would be taken. The three days passed but no one turned himself in. Then the Germans showed their force. They picked up 100 innocent men as hostages, lined them up against a wall on a busy street in Amsterdam, and shot them in cold blood. Many of these murdered men were doctors, scientists, lawyers, and teachers. But that wasn't enough to satisfy them. They also imposed a fine of 15 million guilders (about 5 million dollars at the time) and they didn't care where it came from, as long as it came from the population of Amsterdam. Everyone had to give his share, some doctors were ordered to give an entire year's income.

One clear night, February 12th, 1943, there was a full moon. I said to my parents: "This would be a great night for the English to bomb Germany." No sooner had I said this when we heard the sound of roaring coming from above. We went out on our balcony, looked up, and sure enough, the sky was full of British bombers. The Germans didn't bother to sound the air raid alarm anymore; they didn't care if we got killed; that would just leave fewer people to feed. By this time, we realized that the Americans went on their bombing missions during the day, and the English at night. The Germans put all the searchlights on in the hope of spotting some of those planes. Most of the time they didn't succeed at this, but this time luck was with them. One searchlight singled out one plane and when this was accomplished, all the other searchlights concentrated on that plane. Then they sent up a group of German fighter planes and attacked. I knew it was doomed. But, because it is human nature, I couldn't keep my eyes off this terrible sight. After a vicious attack by these fighter planes, when I could see the bullets flying in the light from the searchlights, the British plane caught on fire. The Germans still didn't stop firing, even though it was already going down. Then I saw three men parachute out of the plane; it was painful to watch, but I couldn't help myself. I was thinking: "Are those boys wounded? Where are they going to land? What will the Germans do with them if and when they catch them?" I went to bed but couldn't sleep, as I was still thinking about those heroic men.

The next evening came the time the English radio was going to give its weekly broadcast in Dutch. (Some of us had not turned in our radios, which was very dangerous.) We listened, and couldn't believe our ears when those very same pilots that had been shot down the night before, came on the air. My mother translated for me as they thanked the Dutch underground for getting them out of Holland. They didn't mention any names, as that would have meant certain death for those who were involved in the escape. We all felt good about this, and proud of our underground.

Another similar incident happened one afternoon when a group of American planes flew over Amsterdam on their way to Germany to do their part to shorten the war. The Krauts had sent up a number of fighter planes and they again managed to isolate one of the American bombers. They kept firing at him, until finally smoke came out and the bomber was out of control. Just prior to going into a nose dive, we saw a parachute open up. They kept right on firing at that poor flyer who was hanging totally helpless from his parachute. We could only hope that he was dead by the time he reached the ground.

As things were getting worse, so were the minds of the people, and every day we would hear about more and more suicides. I saw people jumping from bridges. Others took poison or slashed their wrists, others would turn on the gas.

One of the world's most famous diamond factories was located in Amsterdam (owned by Jews) not far from my house. The Nazis, who were very interested in diamonds for industrial use as well as financially, took the place over one day. Since almost all the people who worked there were Jewish and experienced diamond cutters and polishers, the Germans allowed them to remain and work. They kept them there until there were no more diamonds left to be worked on. Then they were all arrested, together with their families, and transported to Poland.

Because my Dad had been active in the Boy Scouts most of his life, and I had become old enough to join, I became very interested. Somehow we found a troop that was still willing to take Jewish boys.

I joined, studied and was initiated. We met every Saturday afternoon in a "club house" (more like an abandoned shack) near the Parnassusweg, a residential street in the new section of Amsterdam. I enjoyed it, never missed a meeting, and earned several merit badges. But then Hitler decided it was high time that the Boy Scouts became outlawed; after all, this was an organization that had been founded by an Englishman. The "moffen" put out orders that this organization was to disband immediately and no more meetings were permitted, in secret or otherwise. They urged all Dutch (non-Jewish) youth to join their "glorious" movement, the Hitler Youth. Most of the children I knew refused, but some did join. They thought it was the thing to do, and they had nice uniforms. Saturday afternoons they would march through the main streets of Amsterdam, hoping to attract more members, but it didn't do much good. It was silly to see eight year old boys walking around with pistols and big knives, but they needed them for their protection. Every time they paraded, there was lots of fist fights and rock throwing.

Not long after the Boy Scouts were outlawed, its founder, Lord Baden Powell, died. In a roundabout way we were notified that we would have a secret meeting in our troop leader's house, but of course we had to be careful. We were told to come alone, and were all assigned a certain time to arrive, each at five minute intervals, or the neighbors might get suspicious and tell the Gestapo that "there was something going on". After mourning the death of our founder, we discussed the possibility of continuing to meet in secret, as well as doing something for the resistance and underground. I was assigned to run errands and deliver packages. As I didn't have to wear a Jewish star, I was allowed to use the trains, and no one would suspect a boy on a train who was carrying a package.

I never knew what was in those packages. I would get phone calls early in the morning, never knew from whom, as we never used names; and would be told to go to a certain address in the city. I would ring the doorbell, and give a password to whomever opened the door, such as "What a beautiful day it is today," or "Vegetables are difficult to come by." Then I would catch a train and deliver the package, usually to some small village outside of Amsterdam. I think I was bringing money and falsified ration cards to addresses where they hid Jews. I felt very proud and important, that I, little Barry, was doing his part to help the "cause."

About one block from my house lived Jennie, who was in my class, who had a very pretty sister, four years older, Nannie. She was seventeen at the time. We, Jews, were no longer permitted to enjoy or participate in any kind of sports. Nannie lived right on the Amstel, and had always been a lover of all sports; her favorites were swimming and canoeing. One lovely afternoon, she could not resist the temptation; she tore off her Jewish star and rented a canoe. She was seen in her canoe by some people who knew her, and knew she was Jewish. They called Gestapo headquarters and reported her. When she returned the canoe, they were waiting for her, and threw her in jail for 14 days. She lived on bread and water all that time, and was brutally treated. She was also raped several times by the prison guards.

On April 2nd, 1943, my grandmother was notified to be ready at 2 o'clock that afternoon to be deported. It is perhaps hard to believe that this news came almost as a relief, as we had been waiting for it to happen for so long. It is almost like a criminal on the run, constantly in fear of getting caught. Then when they finally catch him, it is a load off his mind. My grandmother didn't want to worry us, but she phoned us anyway to say goodbye.

My parents and I went over to her house immediately and helped her pack. No one said a word; what could we say? The quiet was almost deafening. It wasn't as though we were helping her pack to go on a vacation. None of us knew what was waiting for her, but we all suspected that we would never see her again. Even my mom, who never was close to her, was visibly touched and upset. I didn't know what to do or what to say. How do you say goodbye to your one and only grandparent, who you love so much? This small, kind woman of 65, who did no harm to anyone? What did the Nazis want with her? At 2 o'clock sharp, the Grune Polizei came to her door to arrest her, like a common criminal. We were ordered to leave, and a few days later, we received a letter from her that she had arrived in Westerbork and she was "fine."

Loading the cattle cars for Auschwitz and death.

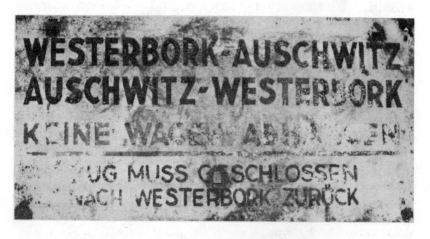

Plaque used on cattle cars, telling railroad workers that these cars are to be used ONLY between Westerbork and Auschwitz and back.

VII. APRIL IN WESTERBORK

Four days after my grandmother had been deported, April 6th, 1943, I had gone to bed just like any other night, not realizing that this would be the last time I would ever sleep in my own bed. It was my mother's turn to stay up, just in case there was a knock on the door, she could answer immediately. This was to be the 14th time they had come for us, but this time it was different...it was the *last* time. I was awakened out of a deep sleep, as our front door was kicked in. I got out of my warm bed and ran into the living room, saw my parents facing two men in civilian clothes, and my Mother arguing with them. As they were not in uniform, which they usually were, and I had never seen them before, I had no idea what was going on. My Dad pulled me aside and gently explained to me that they had come to get us. I said to him: "What about my American papers? You promised me that they would keep us free!" He answered: "They told me that they were picking up all the Jews tonight who have foreign papers. This is not a wild razzia, they have a list of people, and we are on this list. They also said that this meant something good, that we are special people and will be treated accordingly." They gave us ten minutes to pack, but how much could we pack in such a short time? Those ten minutes flew by; we were allowed to take one small suitcase each. It all went so fast that it is hard to recall my exact feelings of what the future would be. I realized we would never be back in our apartment; and walking out of my bedroom, seeing my bed, toys, and books for the last time, to just leave them there, was a very difficult thing to do. My father and I went along with them willingly, especially after what they had told us, but my mother was different. She got excited and started to argue with them, calling them all sorts of names. I had mixed emotions as I watched her. On the one hand I was proud that she had the guts to stand up to them; but on the other hand, I was afraid that they would get angry, pull out a pistol and shoot her, which had happened to other people.

While we were packing, they walked through the house, opened all our closets and helped themselves to food, my father's cigars from his desk, and a few antique silver items still in the house. All during this my Dad seemed calm, just as he had always been, but I was sure he was eating up inside. He was too dignified to show it and give them the pleasure of seeing that he was upset. This reaction may also have been for my benefit to reassure me that we had nothing to worry about.

Then they pushed us out of our home. As we were going down the stairs, I took a last look and saw one of the men locking and sealing our front door. That was the end of our home, the home we had lived in for over ten years, the home my parents had worked so hard for all these years, the home we were so proud of. The center of our lives was gone, and there was nothing we could do.

As we reached the street, a chill hit me; it was a cold night. We were forced to walk a half hour at gunpoint, and taken to a cold, dark and dirty air raid shelter. This made my mother upset, and again she began to yell at the men who had taken us there. They told her, in Dutch; to our surprise, "Vuile rot jood, houw je grote mond" (Dirty lousy jew, shut your mouth). We had been arrested by our own countrymen; something my mother found even harder to take. My father tried to calm her down, telling her that all this didn't do any good; in fact, it might make it even worse.

After we had been there a while, more people were brought in, and we learned that they had Latin-American

76

papers. After a cold and uncomfortable hour passed, a large truck came to bring us to our next prison, the Hollandsche Schouwburg, the regular gathering place in the old Jewish section of Amsterdam. When we walked in, we found about 500 people laying on the floor trying to get some sleep. Some of them had been there for more than two weeks. It was very depressing to see these people on the floor, most of whom were unable to sleep. We found a couple of blankets and located a few square feet of unoccupied space on the floor. I lay down; and in spite of the circumstances, I soon fell asleep from total exhaustion.

I was awakened by my father about eight o'clock that morning, and he offered me some coffee (black hot water) which was our breakfast. It was the worst tasting liquid I had ever had. The whole place smelled as there were no windows, it was overcrowded, and no fresh air. The rest of the day we just sat there doing nothing.

The next day, an announcement was made that all children under 15 were permitted to go for a walk for a half hour once a day. Of course, there were several adults with us to make sure we would come back. The thought of escaping occurred to me during these walks, but where would I go? I had no money, no identity papers, and I couldn't think of anyone who would be willing to put me up, nor could I think of anyone I would want to live with. It was also unthinkable for me to be away from my parents. If I did think of escape, the thought of what they would do to my parents quickly changed my mind. My mother had my New York City birth certificate, as well as the document from the Swiss consul that we were being considered for an exchange. Without me, the papers would be useless.

Then some news broke through; there was going to be a transport of foreign Jews to a transit camp. About 12 o'clock that afternoon we were told to report with our papers to the balcony of the theatre. An administration office had been set up in the balcony by the Joodse Raad (Jewish Advice Bureau). They told us we would soon be leaving for Westerbork. After three hours, we heard an announcement on the microphone: "Family Spanjaard report downstairs to the lobby with their baggage at once!"

We reported to the lobby, to some clerks behind a long table. We told them our name and they gave us registration papers along with a travel permit. We noticed that our papers had a big red "S" stamped on them. We assumed this represented the first letter of our last name, but when we saw the papers of other people, they did not have any letter on theirs. Then we thought it must mean "SPECIAL," because of my American citizenship. But my Dad said...as he knew German fluently, that it meant "Straffe," (penalty or punishment). We were now very worried.

We were then loaded onto big trucks and taken to the train. When we got there, some people from the Joodse Raad came to talk to each of us and pick up our house keys. When a Jewish girl came and asked if we had any messages for anyone, my mother showed her our papers with the big red "S" and asked her about it. The girl's facial expression dropped as she said, "This is no good! What have you done to get this? Did you perhaps give the men who arrested you a difficult time?" Now we knew that this was the result of the argument and name-calling my mother had done. My father knew what it meant, as he had been in Westerbork, and what they did with people who were to be punished.

The girl, still looking very concerned, looked around carefully to see if there was anyone listening and said, "When you get about fifty kilometers outside of Amsterdam, tear the registration papers in tiny pieces, burn them, and throw them through the toilet drain." We thanked her for her helpful suggestion.

After a half hour the train whistle blew, and we pulled out of the station. It was sad leaving Amsterdam, especially under these conditions. As far as we knew, it would be the last time we would ever see it. The train was guarded by men of the Grüne Polizei with loaded rifles and dogs; to make sure we couldn't escape.

My mother said, "What are we going to say in Westerbork when they ask us for our registration papers?" At first none of us knew the answer, but soon Mother came up with a solution. "I'll just tell them that I got sick on the train and fainted, and when I came to, the papers were gone." We thought it was a terrific idea, if it would work.

In the meantime, it got dark, and we couldn't see a thing, as there were no lights in or outside the train. I had to go to the bathroom, but had trouble finding my way. I managed to struggle to the other end of the car, and a strong light came toward me. I was frightened, and imagined myself on the floor after being shot for trying to escape. The light came closer and closer until I finally could recognize a German uniform. Then I was really scared. Before I knew it, he was standing about a foot away from me. He talked calmly. I didn't know if I was dreaming or not; it was the first time I had ever heard a German soldier talk that way. I figured out what he was saying, "Hast du angst?" ("Are you scared?") I shook my head, "yes." Then he told me: "Du brauchst doch kein angst zu haben." (There is no need for you to be scared.) That was easy for him to say, and I thought he was crazy. He walked away and joined his comrades; I no longer needed to go to the bathroom.

I rejoined my parents, and asked them if we had gone fifty kilometers yet. My mother was extremely nervous, but got the courage to take the papers to the bathroom, and do as that girl had suggested. She was gone about fifteen minutes when we started to get worried about her. Maybe one of the guards had caught her. Maybe she really was sick and had passed out. Another five minutes went by, but it seemed more like five years...

In the meantime, my father wrote some letters to some good friends of ours telling them what had happened, and asked them to send us some packages. This is how he "mailed" them. He threw them out the window of the train, hoping that some good people would find them and mail them. They were mailed, and we received many packages as a result of these letters.

Finally, my mother returned with a relieved look on her face and we knew that everything had gone well. We asked her what she had been doing all this time, as we were very worried about her. She replied, "I burned the papers like the girl told me. Then I dropped the pieces through the toilet hole. As you know, this then falls right onto the railroad tracks, and I was afraid someone might find them. So I dropped them carefully one piece at a time, over an area of about ten kilometers." This was very clever of her, but we were still concerned about arriving in Westerbork without registration papers.

I asked my father for the time and he told me it was midnight, and we would be there in about an hour. He knew, as he had been there less than a year ago. He was right; at one in the morning on April 9th, 1943, we could see the lights of the camp ahead of us. The train slowed down until it came to a complete stop, yet we were still some distance from the camp. I saw the Grüne Polizei who had escorted us from Amsterdam, get off the train, and replaced by S.S. men. Later on I found out that the Nazis never permitted escorts to enter any concentration camps so they would *never* discover what went on inside them.

The train moved again, and a few minutes later it came to a complete stop...we had arrived at Westerbork, surrounded by barbed wire, guard towers, armed guards. A choking feeling came over me; there was no turning back, the doors of freedom had closed behind us. My life was no longer my own, we were to be locked up; there was no escape, a feeling of entrapment and hopelessness. My life would now be completely controlled by other people, no longer my parents. No longer could I leave the house whenever I wanted to. No longer could I play in the streets of my neighborhood in Amsterdam with my friends. No longer could I eat whenever I wanted to. I was getting so homesick for my own bed, my house, my neighborhood, my classmates; all the things I had always taken for granted. I held onto my dad's hand as we were ordered out of the train; no one was talking; a chapter in our lives had closed....

We saw men wearing armbands who seemed to be prisoners themselves. Their armbands read, "Joodse Raad." They carried our baggage for us. In the distance we saw the well-lit registration building where we were to go. The three of us stuck together as much as possible. It was our first experience standing in line for hours, outdoors in the cold. I hadn't slept at all that night, and was tired, but there was no place to sleep. We waited three hours in line and, what made it worse, it started to snow. I was half frozen when we finally reached the entrance of the registration building. We, thank God, had warm clothes on, but some other people who were not as fortunate, fainted from the cold and the long wait. Finally, inside where it was warm, I felt better. It took me quite a while to warm up and to stop shaking from the bitter cold.

We were directed to a long table where we found a friendly Jewish girl with a typewriter. We discovered that everything inside the camp was handled by German Jews. She asked us, "May I have your registration papers, please?" Here is where my mother's dramatic ability was put to good use, and she really came through for us. With trembling voice, she explained to the girl that she had gotten very ill on the train, had passed out, and when she came to, the papers were gone. She must have done a very convincing job, as the girl almost started to cry, and answered, "Don't worry, Mrs. Spanjaard, we'll just give you and your family some new ones." What a relief it was to get new registration papers without that feared "S."

We now had to carry our own bags. I was so exhausted; I had enough trouble carrying my own weight, let alone all this luggage. From there we were taken to the office of Lippmann and Rosenthal. My father knew from past experience that everything of value would be taken away there, so he gave me his watch, which was quite valuable, and told me to put it on my arm above my elbow. My mother hid her engagement and wedding rings. After again standing in a long line, it became our turn to get robbed of all our possessions. We were asked to put our hands over our heads by Dutch Nazis. They didn't want to touch us, as they were afraid we had lice, which we didn't, having just left nice clean homes in Amsterdam, but they had been told all Jews had lice.

After we had followed their orders, they couldn't find

anything on us, not even the watch on my upper arm. They seemed disappointed, and must have thought we were poor people. From there they took us to a hospital barrack. The women were sent to one side, and the men to the other side of the building. As we entered a room with a terrible smell, we were told to take off all our clothes. There we were, about fifty naked men and boys. I found it very embarrassing. We walked into the next room and there was a man wearing a white coat. We assumed he was a doctor. He inspected us to see if we had any lice, fleas or other creatures. I was concerned about my Dad's watch I had around my arm, but the doctor didn't seem to notice.

It was five A.M. and the first time in my life I told my father it was time for me to go to bed. After getting dressed, we waited in the hospital building. After a half hour, we were taken to an empty barrack. By this time it had started to get light, and I could easily see the number on the wall. It was painted in large white numbers: "53." We were told to make ourselves as comfortable as possible. We saw dirty beds, stacked three on top of each other, with about two feet of space in between. I couldn't believe we would have to sleep in them.

I flopped down on one of the filthy straw mattresses; but at that point I didn't care, all I wanted to do was get some sleep. As I lay there, I started to think about all the things that happened in the past few days, and suddenly it dawned on me that my Grandmother was somewhere in Westerbork too. My Dad probably had the same thought, but he didn't mention it. She had written us just a few days ago, and the return address on her envelope said she was in barrack No. "63," but I was too tired to do anything about it; I closed my eyes and fell asleep.

I was awakened by my father at eight o'clock; I had slept for just an hour and a half, and was still tired. I asked him why, and he told me that we had been ordered to move to another barrack; none other than No. 63. I got all excited, as now we would get to see my grandmother. I mentioned this to my father (my mom was not with us as she had been sent to the women's side of our barrack), but he didn't seem to be too enthusiastic. There was something wrong, but I didn't know what.

We picked up our things, which we hadn't unpacked as we knew this was not going to be our permanent living quarters. I was very anxious to get to No. 63, but also still tired. To my luck, I found a wheelbarrow outside our building and loaded all our things on it. We could see the barrack come into sight; it was a big wooden structure, painted green. Men and women all around us were going to work. As we entered our new "home," a man was waiting for us; he was the barrack leader. He gave us another registration card as well as another card that would entitle us to receive meals. Then he told us to look for beds "43" and "44." My mother was assigned to the other side of the building in the women's section.

As we entered this long hall, we found about three hundred three-tiered beds all along the walls and several rows of them in the center. They were all made of metal, and each bed had a large dirty burlap bag on them filled with straw. These were to be our mattresses. We found our two beds. In spite of the fact that I was very sleepy, these "beds" looked unappetizing, but I would have to get used to them; as I would have to adjust to so many things in times to come.

Dad then asked me to go to the registration table and ask about Oma (grandma). I went over to one of the men, gave him the name, "Eliseba Spanjaard-Groen," and asked if he knew where she was. He told me he would have to look it up. He looked under the letter "S." His face paled; I knew he had to tell me something I didn't want to hear. He told me, "I am sorry to have to tell you this, but Mrs. Spanjaard was transported to Poland just five hours ago, on the train that left at three o'clock this morning." I thought "We must have passed her somewhere in camp."

I now had to go and tell my father this terrible news. I went back to where our beds were located, and saw that my Dad was already unpacking. By the look on my face, he knew there was something wrong; also, having been here before, he was aware that transports to Poland left every

Tuesday morning. All I could blurt out was: "Oma is gone."* He was silent, continued unpacking, and then changed the subject. I knew my dad, he was suffering inside, as he seldom showed his feelings and kept them to himself.

We tried to make ourselves as comfortable as possible. Many people came over to us to find out what was new in the outside world, as some of them hadn't heard any news in more than a year. We told them all we knew, but it was almost all bad news. The Germans were winning many battles, London was being bombed almost every night; there were not many Jews left in Amsterdam; food, clothing, fuel was getting scarce. All we could do was to try and encourage them, that this could not last forever. Someday the war would be over; the Americans were in it now, and we felt that they were determined to win. This news seemed to cheer them up a bit and give them hope. Even at the age of thirteen, I realized that optimism and hope for the future were the most important ingredients if we were to survive this ordeal.

So, now we were regular tenants of Lager (Camp) Westerbork.

This is the "Who, What, Where and Why" of Westerbork.

WHERE? Westerbork is located about three hundred kilometers northeast of Amsterdam, in the province of Drente, near the city of Assen, about 50 kilometers from the German border.

WHY? In the late 1930's, thousands of Jewish refugees fled from Nazi Germany, many of whom came to Holland, who welcomed them. Some settled in cities throughout Holland and set up businesses. Then came a time when there was no longer any room for them. So the Dutch government built an absorption center for them, called Westerbork. It was set up like a small city. The German refugees were each given a small apartment to live in, about ten to each structure. When the Nazis took over the camp, they broke down all the walls in these buildings, and made barracks out of them. Westerbork was then used as a process center for Holland's 120,000 Jews.

WHAT? This was a so-called "transit" camp. The Ger-

*She was gassed at Sobibor, Poland a few days later.

mans had set this up to take the Dutch Jews they had arrested and process them. Most of the people who arrived there stayed only two or three days before being transported to various "slave labor" camps in Germany and Poland.

WHO? The German Jews who had arrived in Westerbork some years before were the officials of the camp. The outside was guarded and run by the Dutch Military Police, (Marechaussée) under the command of Obersturmführer Albert Konrad Gemmeker of the German S.S. Thus, when the Dutch Jews started to arrive, Westerbork had a German Jewish Commandant, Chief of Police, Chief of Registration, Chief of Labor as well as several doctors and barrack leaders. These people were to remain there the rest of the war. In fact, it was these same German Jews who made up the lists of other Jews who were to be transported to Poland. I realize that had they refused to do this, they themselves would be transported; they had no choice. Anyone in their position would have done the same.

It is ironic, that the same Dutch people who welcomed these German Jews and saved their lives just a few years before, were now at these people's mercy. It was they (the German Jews) whose job it was to see to it that the Germans got 1500, 2000, or 3000 Jews every week. They were also instrumental in sending thousands of innocent men, women and children to their deaths. Because of this, the Dutch Jews had an understandable dislike and mistrust of the German Jews. Because they had managed to receive this authority from Commandant Gemmeker, they remained in Westerbork and survived the war in good shape.

Westerbork was, as far as camps go, not bad. Its purpose was to process Jews. The food was adequate; no one starved. We had heat, medical care and no one was beaten or mistreated. As far as I know, the only people who died there, died of natural causes.

After my Dad and I got settled, I went over to the women's side of the barrack to see how my mother was getting along. She had already unpacked and was getting acquainted with her new neighbors. One of them was Mrs. C.G., who had her four sons and her husband in the camp. I was to become good friends with one of her sons, and spend much time for two years with this family.

I went out to explore the camp, and after discovering that there was no school, I wondered what I was going to do with myself all day, since I had no idea how long we were going to be there.

I also found some interesting things: there were a total of 73 barracks (for living) all together. The entire camp was surrounded by barbed wire. Outside the camp were watch towers with armed guards and spotlights. These guards belonged to the Dutch Military Police, and were forced by the Germans to guard the camp. There were 100 Dutch guards and all but two of them were decent. Most of them didn't like what they were doing, but it was a job they had been assigned to, and they were just following orders. Two of them belonged to the Dutch Nazi Party (N.S.B.) and were devout anti-semites. They all lived in barracks outside the camp, and of course their quarters were nicer than ours.

There was a large registration building, an employment building, the office of Lipmann & Rosenthal, a medical clinic, and a large hospital consisting of ten barracks, all of them behind barbed wire. The camp had a blacksmith, a metal workshop, a carpentry shop, a large drill field, which was sometimes used for soccer games, as well as The Grote Zaal (the grand hall), where we were to have shows and boxing matches. Altogether, it was large.

Then I came upon a single barrack surrounded by barbed wire, with armed guards in front. This was the so-called "S" barrack, (straffe) for penalty. All the people here had shaven heads, wore prison uniforms, and were working outside with an armed guard right over them. I was told that they received very little food and were treated badly. I couldn't help but think how close my family had been to being put in this barrack...the thought alone was frightening.

The average population of the camp was 5000. Sometimes there would be large transports coming in for processing, and then there would be about 15,000 inmates. This happened quite often as they were doing a thorough job rounding up Jews still left in Holland. I remember when one enormous transport came in one night, and there wasn't enough room for them, so they just put 1000 of them in one barrack that was built to hold 400. Imagine what that must have been to endure. These people lived like animals, and a few days later they were put on a transport for Poland.

The remaining men were put to work immediately. Two days after our arrival, my father was digging ditches. It was exhausting for him, as he wasn't used to doing hard labor. Once in a while they would permit me to go where he was working, to bring him some food or water. He would point out doctors, lawyers and teachers also doing this.

At that time, the camp was not too bad, at least it was livable. The worst of it was that our freedom had been taken away. We received some packages from Gentile friends in Amsterdam, which helped. I also received some packages from my classmates who were still left in the Jewish school, with some cheese, bouillon cubes, cookies, and even pancakes, which had been put together at great sacrifice. At night my Dad would put a little pot of water on the pot-belly stove in our barrack, and we would share a cup of delicious bouillon. Some of the women in our barrack worked in the camp kitchen and would steal potatoes. If they managed to get enough of them, they would give one to us. We would then slice them, skin and all, stick them onto the hot stove... when they fell off, they were done; and we had our own home-made potato chips.

Mom and Dad's last picture together
May, 1942

Hollandsche Schouwburg (Dutch Theatre)
First stop after our arrest

Prisoners in courtyard, Hollandsche Schouwburg

Picture, taken secretly, of removal of Jewish
belongings

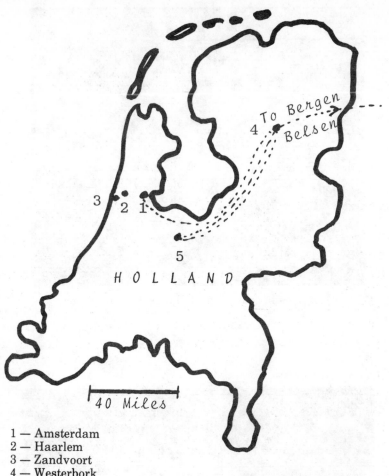

To Bergen
Belsen

4

3
2 1

5

HOLLAND

40 Miles

1 — Amsterdam
2 — Haarlem
3 — Zandvoort
4 — Westerbork
5 — Amersfoort

On left, S.S. Commandant
of Westerbork, Gemmeker.
On right, Aus der Fünten,
Chief of Grune Polizei

VIII. HOTEL AMERSFOORT

Soon the packages stopped coming, as our friends also had been arrested. Westerbork was no paradise, but it was going to get much worse. Then rumors started to go around the camp; all the people with foreign papers were going to be sent to the Amersfoort concentration camp. This worried all of us, as this was a political prison camp for people who had sabotaged the German regime or had dealt in the black market. It was run completely by the S.S. Why would they send us there?

The rumors were true; we were to leave that night. We had to pack again, and report at midnight on the drill field. It was a beautiful night with a full moon. As we got to the field, there were already about 200 people who also were going to be transferred to Amersfoort (also in Holland, in the province of Utrecht, in the middle of Holland and about 40 kilometers from Amsterdam). Oh, how close, and yet so far!

We had to wait about three hours, but it wasn't too bad, as it wasn't cold. It was in the middle of May, one month after we had arrived. At three o'clock in the morning we were told to board a train that was waiting for us. To my surprise, it was a regular train, a passenger train, not the usual cattle cars the Germans always used for transports that were leaving Westerbork. We all wanted to know why we were being sent to Amersfoort, and soon one of the men from the camp administration came over and explained that we had to make room for some large transports they were expecting. Hitler was about to keep his promise to make Europe "Juden rein" (clean of Jews), and was about to embark on the largest and final sweep of any remaining Jews in Holland; those still in Amsterdam, as well as those who had gone into hiding.

The train pulled out of Westerbork, and I tried to make myself as comfortable as possible, but this was very difficult, as the train was overcrowded. We huddled together and I soon fell asleep on my Dad's lap. I suddenly woke up when the train had come to a complete stop; we had arrived in Amersfoort. I asked my Dad what time it was, and he told me it was 6 o'clock.

As we were ordered from the train, I found myself in a city with people walking around, free. Oh, how I envied them! Then we were lined up by German S.S. men with large guard dogs; this camp was completely under control of the S.S. They all had German Shepherd dogs, but they didn't look at all like my old "Teddy," these were vicious looking animals who looked like they would just love to take a big bite out of any of us.

After an hour's walk, we reached the camp. As we were approaching, I got the feeling that this was a much stricter one than the one we had just left. There were blood-hound dogs everywhere, and it was completely surrounded by three rows of electrified barbed wire.

The gate was opened, and we walked into our new "hotel." We were ordered to stand in rows of ten on a large open drill field, at attention for three hours. Many people couldn't take it and collapsed. We had received no food or water since our evening meal the night before in Westerbork. Then the commandant of the camp arrived, who we had been waiting for all this time. He stepped on a platform, and barked at us in German. I couldn't understand a word he was saying, but my Dad translated. We were told that we had to be in our barrack by nine o'clock at night, that anyone caught outside after that hour would immediately be shot, no questions asked. At 9:15 everyone had to be in bed, as there would be an inspection and head count.

At exactly ten minutes before nine, a bell rang as a warning, and at nine o'clock another. At that time, German guards came around with loaded rifles to make sure everyone was following orders.

There were two barracks assigned to us, one for the women and children, and one for the men and boys my age. They were opposite each other. They were clean and made out of stone. The barracks in Westerbork were made out of wood, so it looked as though we were in for a somewhat better life. That next day we found out differently.

When I woke up about six o'clock, everyone was already awake, and by the looks on their faces, I could see there was something wrong...One of the men in our group had been shot, and his body was left outside our barrack. The Germans had left it there as an example to us to show what would happen if we were "disobedient."

This "disobedience" was breaking the curfew hour. Because of the bad food we had been given, most of the people had diarrhea. They had to go to the bathroom constantly during the night. It didn't bother me (I guess my stomach was made out of iron). There was only one bathroom for the entire barrack, and when this man went there, he found a long line waiting ahead of him. When his cramps became so severe that he couldn't hold it any longer, he decided to go to another bathroom which was located about 20 yards from our building. He didn't quite make it; he was shot the minute he stepped outside. Everyone of us was ordered to walk around the body five times. It was the first time in my young life I had seen a dead body.

The next day the commandant with some German guards came over to our side of the camp to select a Jewish camp commander. They wanted someone to be responsible to them for everything we did. They also selected barrack leaders, and a man was chosen for the women's barrack. A few nights later, one of the women was not in her bed on time. One of the guards caught her, but didn't say or do anything to her. Instead, he went to the barrack leader, ordered him outside, and made him crawl on his hands and knees around the barrack, until he was told to stop. Since the barracks were very long, the poor man had a very rough time of it. After they finally told him he could stop, after ten trips, he fainted from total exhaustion and was sick for a week. This was a typical German method; they did nothing to the woman who had done "wrong," but punished the leader instead.

Two babies were born there during this time. Naturally, they didn't get the nourishment babies require, but they stayed alive. It is interesting to see what people can stand without much food.

Surprisingly enough, for a camp such as the one we were in, the food was not too bad, but not enough, and I was hungry all the time.

One afternoon as I was walking through the camp, trying to find something to do, I saw a truck parked in an isolated area. My curiousity got the best of me, so I lifted one of the covers to see what was inside. It was loaded with large cartons of canned beets and sauerkraut. Normally, these are not my favorite vegetables, but I was hungry. I climbed into the truck and grabbed as many cans as I could hold, jumped out of the truck and ran like hell. I invited a couple of my friends, and for the next two days we hid in back of our barrack and ate beets and sauerkraut. We ate so much of it, that to this day I can't stand them.

About two hundred feet from us were barracks that housed the non-Jewish political prisoners. We were all anxious to find out why they were there; but they weren't allowed to talk to us, nor we to them. They wore striped prison suits and shaved heads. Somehow, we found out that most of them had been caught dealing in the black market, and some of them had participated in the resistance movement. They were treated barbarously, much worse than we were.

Every morning at six o'clock all these prisoners had to work outside the camp, digging a rifle range for the Germans. Many afternoons we could hear the sound of rifle and machine gun-fire coming from that direction. We assumed that this was just practice. The truth was that almost daily one of the guards would be assigned to take twenty prisoners to work, but he was then given orders to return with only *five*. Now we knew what the "practice" was, they were using these men as targets.

As the camp was completely surrounded by three rows of electrified barbed wire, anyone touching them would immediately be electrocuted, if he wasn't shot by one of the guards in the towers for just approaching the fence. One day I saw the guards showing our camp to some visiting officials. They decided to have some entertainment and impress their guests at the same time. They ordered one of the political prisoners, a boy about eighteen, to come over. He ran over, took off his cap and stood at attention, at least five feet away from the member of the "Master race," as we had all been ordered to do. They grabbed the boy's cap, threw it onto the barbed wire, then ordered him to get it. He didn't have any choice; he knew if he disobeyed their orders, he would be shot on the spot by the man who had given him the order. On the other hand, if he did go get his cap, maybe the guard in the tower might not see him, or at least would realize what was going on and not shoot. But he was wrong... as soon as he came near the fence, the guard in the nearest tower opened fire and killed him; much to the delight of the German spectators.

It has always been my habit to keep busy. At my age, 13, almost 14 by now, I didn't have to work and the days went by very slowly. Shortly after I got to Amersfoort, I discovered a small building, the camp post office, and went and talked to the man who worked there. He was nice looking, in his early thirties, dressed in good civilian clothes, something I hadn't seen in a while. As he didn't chase me out, I decided that he was safe to talk to. He told me he was in charge of the post office, that he was not a prisoner, but a civilian.

I asked him if I could help him, to have something to do to kill time. He agreed; so from then on, about three o'clock every afternoon I worked in this little post office, mostly sorting out packages that had come in. Under his supervision, I would open the packages to see if there were any illegal items, such as weapons or liquor. I appreciated this opportunity to work, although the pay was bad (none), but it helped to fill my days.

Exactly one month from the day we arrived, we left, June 6th, 1943, and were returned to Westerbork. We were told to pack everything we had, and be ready at 6 o'clock that evening. The sun was still out, as it was summer, and we were happy to leave this camp. As usual, we had to walk to the railroad station again, but I didn't mind it, as it was a nice walk. We went right through the city of Amersfoort. If one of us had been smart (or is it dumb?) or quick enough, he could have jumped to the side, and mingled with the civilians who were standing on the side of the road watching . No one did, as all of us would have suffered as a result.

IX. TRANSIT LIFE GOES ON

We arrived at the station, and again a passenger train was waiting for us. The service was always free, no waiting, and always on time.

On the way to the station, some people in our group managed to slip some letters to bystanders, and no one was caught. We had to fear being seen by our German escorts, and then there was the chance that a letter given to a stranger might be a member of the Dutch Nazi party, and then there would have been hell to pay.

After a few hours' ride in the train, it was back to Westerbork, "home sweet home." We were taken to barrack No. 73; and were told it was a special barrack for Jews with foreign papers, men married to Gentile women, as well as Jews who had been baptized. Most of these baptized Jews had done so out of self-preservation, rather than religious beliefs. The Germans were aware of this, and if these people had not been baptized before a certain date, it didn't help them. It was a new barrack and in good condition.

The next day I walked around the camp to find out what had happened while we were in Amersfoort. First of all, a lot of transports had come through during the past four weeks. About 10,000 people had been processed and sent on to Poland. About an additional thousand had arrived and been kept in Westerbork for various reasons. I found a lot of old friends I had not seen in a long time, who had arrived while I was away.

There were also many people I knew who had been caught from their underground hiding places, but they were placed in the feared "S" barrack.

As soon as I found out that a lot of Jews who had hidden had been picked up (most of them because someone had sold them out, for 7½ guilders—about $3), I immediately thought of Ellie, my old girl friend and co-star from Amsterdam. I went to the administration building to inquire about her and her family. Sure enough, their names were listed... they had come and gone while we were away. This pretty and lively little girl, whom I liked so much, was now gone forever, or so I thought at the time.

About five days after we had returned, I thought that it was time I got busy doing something, instead of aimlessly walking around all day. There was no school, and the days dragged on. Before I could do anything about it, I became quite ill with a high fever, and was sick for more than a week. After that, even though I was still very weak, I went to the building where they assigned work, an employment agency, with no fees and no salary. They sent me to the hospital to work as an orderly in the clinic.

My job consisted of cleaning glass microscope slides after they had been used for blood or urine tests. I also cleaned and sterilized test tubes. I had to work hard, but I felt I was doing something useful. Being around doctors and nurses in a hospital setting fascinated me, and I asked my Dad if I might someday become a surgeon, when we were free again. He said this was a fine idea and a noble profession, and would require lots of studying. He said he would do everything in his power to help me reach this goal. I worked there eight months.

One clear, sunny day as I was about to have some lunch, I heard a noise in the sky. This was nothing new to me, because whenever it was nice weather, many American planes flew over our camp on their way to Germany on bombing missions. They had the "day shift" while the English, the "night shift." Normally, the Germans did not shoot at them. Why, I never found out. This time it was

g alone, an easy target
by its size that it was a
l. There were no fighter
red what was going on,
. When I first saw it, it
it came lower and lower,
ke a landing. I couldn't
ne was not on fire and
Suddenly, one of the men
e opened. It came lower and
nen jumped. To my relief, all
the bomber disappeared in the
ating a huge cloud of black smoke.
of excitement and our guards imme-
men in the towers. They were afraid that
eginning of an invasion, and that we, the
s, would now have enough nerve to escape.

I ran to the other side of the camp with everyone else,
and stood near the fence. In the distance I could see a large
white sheet, which must have been a parachute. Then I
saw a car leaving the camp. It was the commandant, with
several soldiers, going to capture the American flyers.
They returned without any of them, and I kept praying
that the underground got there first. I was still afraid that
the flyers didn't get away; as the entire area around the
camp was perfectly flat, and there was no place for them to
hide.

At two o'clock I went back to work at the clinic; but there
was no news about the flyers. The afternoon went by quite
fast, as I had a lot of work to do; and before I knew it, it was
five o'clock, time to go home. I was just about to leave
when I saw a truck driving up towards the operating room,
which was in back of the clinic. I had never seen this truck
before, because it was an ambulance. When it stopped at
the operating room, I went to see who was there. One
American flyer was on a stretcher, and another one walking.
They were the ones who had parachuted from the plane
that morning. I couldn't see the one on the stretcher, as he
was covered with a blanket, but I got a good look at the

99

other one. What a uniform, all in white fur, and I was impressed. How I wished I could speak English, since I was an American-born boy and was dying to be able to say something to him; then he would answer me. That would have been wonderful!

I saw that the soldier on the stretcher was seriously hurt. When I looked at those men I couldn't help but wonder what was awaiting them in a prison camp. They had put their lives on the line in order to go on a mission that perhaps would shorten the war and free people like me. Even though I didn't know them, I felt a real kinship, yes even love for them. I got a lump in my throat and started to cry. I felt tremendous sympathy for them, as they too would now be prisoners. They were the first American soldiers I had ever seen.

As they left the truck, the one who was walking passed about a foot from me. If there had been no barbed wire separating us, I could have touched him.

I walked around the back of the operating room to look through a large window. The doctor and nurses bent over and lifted the blanket from the stretcher. The doctor was a famous and respected Jewish surgeon from Germany, who was also a prisoner. After about five minutes I had to leave, as I heard the commandant was coming to attend the operation.

The next day when I came to work I found out the whole story. The Americans had left England the morning before to bomb Berlin. After they finished their mission, returning to their base in England, they were attacked. The plane didn't receive heavy damage, and could have easily made it home. However, one of the crewmen was hit in his leg with 17 bullets, bleeding heavily, and would have died before reaching home base. The crew decided they would jump, let the plane crash, and surrender; hoping to obtain immediate medical help. The other crewmen were brought to our camp, to donate blood for the operation. The injured American was saved by his buddies who were willing to go to a prisoner of war camp in order to save his life.

They were held in our camp for three days, but in separate quarters. No one was allowed to talk to them, but through the doctor we found out that the wounded flier's leg had been amputated. I often wondered what happened to these heroes, and if they survived the war.

Our German Commandant, Gemmeker, was as camp commandants go, not a bad man. He had been assigned to run Westerbork, which was to be used strictly as a transfer camp. He did just that; he never bothered us, and left the internal running of the camp to the German Jews.

He must have been very bored with his job, as we were. There was no school; it had been tried, but didn't work. There were no books, and the teachers came and went. So, to get rid of us for a few hours, he permitted guarded hikes outside the camp. They didn't have to be afraid we would run away, as the camp was located in the middle of nowhere. The nearest house, except the commandant's private house, was miles away. In the winter we didn't go on these hikes, so there was absolutely nothing for the children to do. My dad was still digging ditches, so I never saw him during the day. My mother was usually not well, so I didn't spend much time with her either.

One day Gemmeker got an idea. In order to relieve his boredom, and keep us busy, he ordered a boxing training school to be run by Dutch boxing champions, Santilhano, Waterman and Bennie Bril, who were prisoners. I did not like boxing, but I joined for the exercise. We did a lot of running, jumping rope and shadow boxing. We also got extra rations of milk, and were permitted to take more showers than the rest of the people. The commandant would regularly come and watch us work out. I liked the training and being around these famous boxers.

Then, to my complete surprise, my trainer told me I was to go in the ring. I hadn't planned on that, and it scared me. My opponent was much stronger than me, and I had a headache for three days.

The commandant enjoyed these bouts. (What good Nazi wouldn't enjoy watching two Jews beat the hell out of each other?) He ordered us to set up a big boxing night. Mr. Bril told me he wanted me in it, so I had to have heavier training. A few days before the "big night," they made the administration building into a boxing arena.

I was assigned to box Jacques G., my best friend, who had a natural instinct for boxing. He even looked like one with his nose flat against his face; it had been broken a few times. Whenever he watched someone else box, it was as though he himself was up there in the ring, and acted out every punch.

Then came the big night, and tension built up, not only in the arena, but throughout the entire camp. Our match was not the only one; there were many others that followed ours, but as far as I was concerned, it was the ONLY one that night. When I climbed into the ring, I felt that this was how the Christians in the old Roman days used to fight the lions for the pleasure of the spectators. I looked around as I sat in my corner, waiting for the bell to ring. In the front row sat our "beloved" commandant, Gemmeker and his cohorts. They could hardly wait for the blood to start flowing. Behind them sat my father and mother.

The bell rang, and Jacques immediately started to do a job on me. He wound up his right arm, circled it a few times and landed it on top of my head. The crowd went "ooohhh," but I hardly felt it; after all, we were wearing gloves. It was more the indignity of it that hurt the most. Finally, my mother couldn't take it any longer and started to yell: "Stop beating him!" I was very embarrassed. Jacques, of course, won by a decision, after three rounds. For the next few days every bone in my body and face hurt. Jacques and I then became good friends and spent the rest of our stay in the camps together. The day after the fight, we were given extra food and even real milk as a reward from the commandant, as he had enjoyed the evening.

In our camp was a man who had operated the largest cabaret show in Holland. He was summoned to Gemmeker's office, told to plan for a camp theatre. As we had no theatrical supplies, the commandant permitted him to go to Amsterdam to purchase whatever was needed. His wife and brother were also prisoners and if he decided not to return, immediate transport to Poland would be their punishment.

Four weeks later the show opened. It was so good, it ran for 25 consecutive nights, and every night the commandant sat in the front row. Every barrack was given a certain amount of tickets, so everyone got to see it.

After that, we got a restaurant, but all it had was lemonade and imitation coffee. We had music played by pianists and violinists. It took our minds off our misery for a while.

We were allowed to get packages. If you were lucky enough to receive them, and didn't have to fear transport to Poland, a person could exist in Westerbork. In fact, during the last winter of the war, 1944, it was better in Westerbork than in Amsterdam. The Dutch had no food and no heat.

Quite a few people in the camp had "good" papers, proving that they had been baptized into Christianity; that they were married to non-Jewish people, or that they had fought with the German Army in the First World War. These papers were good enough to keep them from the extermination camps in Poland. The trouble was that they didn't have them with them. If they told the commandant that they possessed these documents in Amsterdam, he would give them permission to go get them. They had to sign statements swearing that they would return. Everything went well, until one day a woman didn't come back. My Dad had just got permission to go to Amsterdam to get valuable papers for me. He was about to leave when an announcement was made that all permits had been cancelled because someone had not returned.

This proved to be very harmful to us, as we never did get these papers. If we had, we would have been sent to Vittel in Southern France, a hotel where they kept people under house arrest for the duration of the war.

All the men and women over the age of 15 had to work. The women were assigned to the kitchens and did the cooking. The British had dropped ammunition for the resistance, but in many cases the Germans found it, and wanted to store it in our camp. Our commandant didn't want to take a chance that it would blow up, so he ordered bunkers to be built outside the camp.

Every day more and more transports came in, consisting of Jews who had been caught in their hiding places all over the country. Once a week, a large transport came from Amsterdam consisting of people who had been picked up in razzias.

Tuesday had been set aside for transports to Poland, and these would leave early in the morning, with 1000 to 5000 people, depending on how the Nazis felt. On Monday afternoon, Gemmeker, the same man who had given us our theatre and boxing, would come over to the leaders of the camp and instruct them to get the ordered amount of Jews ready for transport the next morning. He didn't care if they were children, old, or sick. He demanded a certain number of people. The German Jews now had to make up lists of their fellow Jews to be deported to God knows where or what. It was bad enough to be a prisoner, but at least we were still in our own native country, and this gave us a secure feeling. The idea of being shipped off in the middle of the night to some foreign country, made us feel hopeless, helpless and completely cut off from our familiar surroundings.

There were railroad tracks running through the middle of the camp. Monday nights the cattle-cars were brought right into the area; sometimes the train would be so long that the end of it would be outside the camp. On the cars had been painted the words, in French: "Huit Cheveaux/ Quarante Hommes" (eight horses or forty people). The Germans didn't pay attention to this, as they usually would shove 80 or more people into them. The trip to Poland took three days, and the people had to stand up all the way, with no food, water, air, or bathroom facilities. Usually, at least half the people would be dead by the time they arrived at their destination.

My mother told me the story of a 96 year old woman, who was in the cot next to her in the hospital. She was a tiny, fragile, typically Jewish old lady. One Tuesday morning, the transport list was read off in the hospital barrack. It was four in the morning, and the people whose names had been called were told to be ready to leave at eight. This woman's name was on the list. Her son, an eye specialist, was also in the camp; and when he heard that his mother was to be transported that morning, he immediately came to her bedside. With tears in his eyes, he told her: "Mammelle, I have tried everything, but I can't do anything for you. There is just no way I can get you off this list." Then the head nurse came into the hospital barrack, and announced that it was time for the people who had been called that morning to report to the train. The young doctor bent over, picked up his little mother, and carried her all the way to the waiting cattle-cars. He was crying uncontrollably, but she seemed to be more resigned, and tried to console him. She was so brave; at least, she appeared so. When my mother told me this story, we both cried. We realized that this old woman probably did not survive the trip to Poland.

One of the most moving and courageous things occurred every Tuesday morning. As the cattle trains pulled slowly out of Westerbork, with the doors slammed shut and sealed, could be heard hundreds of voices singing the "Hatikvah"* from inside the cars. Those of us who remained in Westerbork were always moved by this. We were also grateful that we were not the ones on the train, and were permitted to stay. At that time, most of us felt that we would probably remain there until the liberation; although many of us felt this might never come.

All the lights in the barracks had to be out by 10:30, but some of us young adults who did not have to work didn't want to be in bed so early. One night we took a few suitcases to the washrooms where the lights were allowed to be on all night and, sat down to play cards. All went well until about two in the morning when we heard footsteps coming towards us. The door opened slowly, and there in front of us was none other than Gemmeker himself. He was in civilian clothes and none of us recognized him at first. As

*The Jewish national anthem.

soon as we did, we all were frightened, because what we were doing was a criminal offense. This man had the power to do anything he wanted with us. He stood there for a few minutes, staring at us coldly, turned around, and left without saying a word. We would have liked it better if he had said something. What did happen was that our barrack leader heard about it and punished us. For two weeks we had to clean the outside of the barrack. Gemmeker could have made things much worse for us.

Holland's favorite outdoor sport was soccer. In the camp was Han Hollander, a famous sportscaster. When Holland played Germany for the World Cup before the war, he went to Germany to give the radio report. Hitler was in power at that time, and thought Mr. Hollander had done an outstanding job reporting the game. Not knowing that he was Jewish, he personally gave him a medal.

When Mr. Hollander was arrested and sent to Westerbork, he was given special treatment because of that medal. He didn't have to live with the other prisoners inside the camp; he was in the barracks with the Marechaussée (Dutch military police). He was safe, and didn't have to fear transport to Poland. He remained there for about ten months until one Monday night he got in trouble with a drunken German soldier, who started to call Mr. Hollander anti-semitic names. The sportscaster got angry and beat him up, and he broke the soldier's arm. The next morning he was put on the regular Tuesday morning transport, medal and all; and as far as we know, he never returned.

One day, Gemmeker visited a nearby city, Assen, driven by a Jewish prisoner who had been his chauffeur for three years. On their return, the driver lost control of the car and they crashed into a tree. The driver was not hurt, but Gemmeker's leg was broken. He was taken to our camp hospital, and demanded to see the same doctor who had treated the American flyer. After the doctor was through setting his leg, the commandant told him that he was going to reward him. If the doctor was sent to the gas chambers, he would see to it that he would get a heavy dose of gas, so that he would die faster. Some reward! This is the mentality of the S.S. On one hand, here was a man who gave us boxing, theatre, a restaurant; on the other hand, he was perfectly capable of making this type of vicious remark.

In the beginning, we were allowed to receive as many packages as we could get. This was not easy. Even if we were lucky enough to still know some people who were free, they had tremendous food shortages. When the commandant thought we were getting too many of them, he started a new system of control. We were given stamps, which we sent to the people on the outside. They would then put these stamps on the outside of the parcels, otherwise, the Germans would keep them.

We were permitted to write one letter every two weeks, as well as two postcards. The cards were ordinary postcards, but the letters had to be on special camp stationery, and were always censored. We were not allowed to put stamps on them, the Germans did this after they had read them, and for good reason. Some people were smart enough to write a whole letter underneath the stamps.

Many days I would just wander around the camp, aimlessly, alone, bored, feeling hopeless, depressed and sorry for myself. Many questions would run through my mind; such as, what was to become of us? Would the war ever end? Suppose the Germans won? Would we EVER get out? How long would we be able to stand this kind of life? And what about my education?

I missed the good old days in Amsterdam, when I wasn't hungry and afraid; when I was just a happy boy, looking forward to my Dad coming home from work, eating a nice dinner. In the evening my Dad and I would play a game of backgammon or dominos. He had such patience with me, and I missed all this so much. Now my Dad came back to the barracks, hungry and exhausted. I'm sure, although he never said it, he felt helpless and frustrated that his family was in this situation and there was NOTHING he could do about it. A man's natural instinct is to provide for his wife and family, but he was not doing so. He must have felt very guilty about it.

The highlight of my week was on Sundays when he and I would take a walk through the camp and talk. I recall when he told me, "Barry, when this is all over, and it will be, I will see to it that you and Mommy will never be hungry again; and I will make sure you will get a good education, because without it you will never amount to anything. You have a good mind and it is very possible that you could become a good lawyer or doctor." I loved listening to him, he knew that my secret desire was to be a surgeon, but now it all seemed so impossible. I loved him so much that if he had asked me to become a mountain climber, I would have done so—just to please him.

One night, the Commander of the Grune Polizei, Aus der Fünten, visited our camp with a miserable message. There were about one hundred Jewish men who had married Gentile women, who were told to report to the registration building. After waiting an hour, someone yelled: "ACHTUNG!" Everyone immediately snapped to attention. Aus · der Funten, in typical Nazi fashion entered the hall, followed by many high ranking officers. He arrogantly walked onto the stage that had been built for him, and announced the reason he had "honored" them with his presence. He promised that all these men could return home, IF... they would report to a hospital in Amsterdam to be sterilized. If they signed a document agreeing to this now, they could return to their homes that very evening. If they didn't, they would be sent to a concentration camp in Poland on the next transport. I don't know how many went home that night, but one of them who lived in our barrack chose to take his chances and remain, and not be disfigured. None of us knew what happened to the thousands of people who were transported to Poland, but we imagined they had a fifty-fifty chance. The man who decided not to return to his home was deported the following Tuesday and never came back.

One day, on an errand for my mother about a mile away from our barrack on the opposite side of the camp, I saw a truck pass by. As it was hot, I thought I could hitch a ride. I ran and grabbed onto the back, and hung on for dear life. It suddenly picked up speed and before I knew it, I was past the guardhouse and outside the camp. Immediately, one of the guards came running out and told the driver to stop.

He ordered the driver to back up and stop in front of the guardhouse. As I jumped off the truck, he came over to me and I could see in his eyes that he was very angry. As far as he was concerned, I was trying to escape. I was shaking all over. He shoved me inside the guardhouse and told me to stand in the corner until he told me otherwise. I stood there for about an hour, but it seemed more like a year. Crazy things went through my mind. I knew the penalty for trying to escape. What if they sent me to Poland without ever seeing my parents again? What if they decided to leave me standing there forever with no food or water? Maybe they would even shoot me as an example to the other prisoners for trying to escape. I was terrified.

Finally, the guard angrily told me to go to my barrack and get my father or mother to bring my camp registration card. He sent an orderly with me, to make sure that I would return. This time I was even more scared than before, because now my parents were going to know about it. When I reached our barrack, my mother was there, as my dad had already left for work. On the way, I tried to explain to her what had happened. As we entered the guardhouse, the guard came over to talk to her. He seemed to have changed in that half hour; he was very polite to my mother. He told her that we were very lucky that he had been on duty at the time, because if one of the "bad" guys had been there, he would have reported me to the commandant, and who knows what would have happened then? He warned me never to do such a thing again. My mother was grateful to him for letting me off so easily. Then we left.

On the way back to our barrack she bawled me out. I don't know if she was more angry about the fact that I got "caught trying to escape," or that I never did do the errand for her. When my mother got mad, she could really let you have it.

Another woman who could really let you have it, only with her it was more of a permanent nature, was Frau

Slottke, a high ranking Nazi, whose job was to travel to all the concentration camps to check if all the Jews were being deported fast enough. One Tuesday we had the "honor" of a visit from her. We received a notice saying that the Spanjaard family was to report to the registration building at eight o'clock that night with all our papers and documents. None of us said anything on the way, but we were all thinking the same thing: "This was the end of us."

After our regular dinner, which consisted of hot water called soup, we prepared to go to the registration building. We got our papers together. The most important one was a copy of my American birth certificate; I never did have my own American passport. The trouble was that a certificate of birth from a country is not necessarily proof of citizenship. In Holland I was considered 100% Dutch, as I was the son of a Dutchman. The Americans considered me 100% American, because I was born there, so I carried what is called: "Dual Nationality." This was rather ironic, because there were millions of people throughout Europe who were considered "Statenlose" (stateless), as Hitler had taken away their citizenship, and here I was with *two* nationalities. The only way of having solid proof of citizenship is a passport; but unfortunately, I did not have one. So this was a very "iffy" situation: Would the German High Command in Berlin consider me American or not?

As we entered the Registration building, we found twenty people ahead of us who had American or English papers. After an hour, we were called in. We knocked on the door, and a woman's voice said: "Kommen Sie herein" (come in). As we entered, I was shocked by the ugliest woman I had ever seen sitting behind a large desk. There were no chairs where we could sit, so we stood and listened to her talk with a voice like her face. She asked our names, looked at a long list, until she reached ours. I could read what it said, even though it was in German and upside down. The six months of German I had in school came in handy. It said:

Herr Spanjaard, Alfred B.	Niederlander
Frau Spanjaard-Roozeboom, Sophie	Niederlander
Sohn Spanjaard, Barry A.	Amerikaner

She then asked us for our papers, so we gave them to her assistant, who handed them to her. She did not want any direct contact with Jews. She asked us for my passport, and my mother had to tell her that I didn't have one and explained why. Frau Slottke then said: "Well, that's too bad, because now I will have to send you to Poland, instead of an internment hotel in the South of France." We again felt that this was the end of the Spanjaards. Before we left, she told me that I would have to go to one of the other buildings to be fingerprinted.

We went back to our barrack but none of us slept much that night. The next morning my dad took me to the office to have my fingerprints taken. While we were there, we met some people we knew from Amsterdam, who had English or American papers. Naturally, we were eager to find out what Frau Slottke had said to them, as we knew that they were lucky enough to possess passports. She had told them to be ready any minute, as they were going to be sent to an internment camp, called Vitel, a resort hotel in Southern France. One week later, a beautiful passenger train, something we hadn't seen in a long time, arrived and about 15 people got aboard and left. They indeed were taken to Vitel, and later I was to find out that they all survived the war. If my parents had just spent that five dollars back in 1932, in New York, for my American passport, we too would have been on that train. This was, however, not our last encounter with Frau Slottke.

Every day was just about the same as all the other days, and every Tuesday morning, like clockwork, another transport consisting of many cattle (box) cars loaded with men, women and children, would leave our camp for Poland, and Auschwitz. After witnessing these heartbreaking scenes week after week, month and month, we started to get used to them. Every other day small transports of new prisoners came in who had been caught in their underground hiding places. From these sad people we got some of the latest news from Amsterdam, where things were getting worse and it seemed the Germans were winning most of their battles.

About three times a week, if it was clear weather, we could see and hear hundreds of American bombers and fighter planes flying over on their way to Germany or on their way back to England. All this made us feel great and boosted our morale. Sometimes I could see the worried looks on our guards' faces; as, after all, it was *their* wives and children who were in danger. There was little sympathy from us.

My mother went back in the hospital, as she was weak and sick from a bleeding ulcer. She had great difficulty adjusting to confinement. My dad and I did our best to stick it out even though he had to work harder every day, digging seemingly endless ditches. What they were used for, we never knew.

A new fear entered our life; an epidemic of infantile paralysis (polio) broke out. It was carried into the camp by a prisoner, who shortly after arriving came down with the disease. Two more, three more, and then twenty-five people were afflicted. A special quarantined hospital barrack was set up, surrounded by barbed wire. Soon there were about 100 people with polio, a few of whom died. Perhaps it might have been better for these people to die there instead of in the gas chambers of Auschwitz.

We had the honor of seeing Frau Slottke again, when she returned to pay us another visit. It seemed as though she liked our place. What Nazi didn't enjoy the sight of seeing Jews in captivity? We received another note from her requesting the "honor of our company." This is the woman who was described as "a nightmare come to life", who hated children because she had none, who destroyed happiness, a ghastly figure. . . "bat-like."

She said she had some better news for us this time. She instructed us to pack immediately as we were to be transported to the auschtausch lager (exchange camp), Bergen-Belsen. . . .

She sounded like a travel agent, trying to talk us into a vacation trip. I could not figure out why she told us these lies; it wasn't as though she wanted us to "volunteer" to go to Bergen-Belsen; we were, after all, merely cattle in her eyes to be shipped there, and eventually destroyed. She told us how nice Bergen-Belsen was, and how happy we would be. We would have heated barracks made of stone instead of the wooden ones we were living in now, and we would all be together. She said the food was good and she had the gall to tell us that if we so desired, we could have "kosher" food. She made it all sound like the Catskills in New York, and we were ready to book for the entire summer season.

This took place on November 10th, 1943, and we were scheduled to leave on the 16th along with about 200 others. We all packed, looking forward to leaving here for the "privileged" camp. On the 15th, a nice passenger train arrived with about eight cars with a freight car for the baggage. Everyone who was scheduled to go on this transport was ordered to put their baggage in this car. By that evening we were all ready. However, the next morning we received notice that this transport was a mistake. We removed all our belongings from the train and returned to our barracks. They promised that some day this transport would take place. Yes, someday, but when.... We were all disappointed when we went back to our already overcrowded living quarters.

Soon New Years Eve arrived: it was to be our first one in captivity, there were no celebrations, and it came and went almost unnoticed.

An unusual discovery in 1983 at the War Documentation Bureau in Amsterdam: Westerbork children circa 1943 Author on extreme right.

X. BERGEN-BELSEN; THE CHOSEN FEW

The first transport to Bergen-Belsen took place the beginning of January, and my parents and I were scheduled to be on it. My mother was still in the hospital with bleeding ulcers, so we were taken off the list. I was disappointed; yes, I was even angry with my mother, because it was her fault that we weren't going to this "wonderful" place. Now we were stuck in Westerbork for God knows how long.

On January 31st, 1944, we got a message from the office to pack again and be ready in just ten minutes to be sent to Bergen-Belsen. We didn't have much to pack, but we didn't have time to get our little suitcases out of the storage room. A train rolled up, but this time it wasn't a passenger train; it was a train consisting of seven cattle cars, two of which had some old broken cots for the very ill. My mother was still in the hospital and too weak to walk to the train, so she was carried on a stretcher and placed in the "hospital" car. My father and I wanted to be with her to help her, even though there wasn't much we could do as there were no medicines.

On the outside of each boxcar was written: "8 Cheveaux-40 Hommes" A terrible fear came over us as we approached these horrible vehicles, and we began to understand how all those unfortunate people felt on the regular Tuesday morning transports to Auschwitz. If we were going to such a wonderful camp, why were we being taken there in these ugly boxcars?

There were about ten cots in our car and they took up all the room. The "gentlemen" didn't think that was enough, so they pushed in another 40 people. We couldn't stand; we couldn't breathe, and we couldn't even sit down. Of those 40 people, my dad and I were the only ones who weren't sick. As I looked out, I saw some people put bread, water, and butter in one car. This was supposed to be our rations for the trip to Germany, but we never got it.

Then ten big, uniformed Grüne Polizei, complete with machine guns and police dogs, went from car to car, slamming the doors, locking and sealing them. When they got to the car I was in, and slammed it shut, a trapped feeling came over me. Suddenly, it became totally dark, and we were completely shut off from any fresh air. People all around started to cry and moan. I hung on to my father's hand, as I was sure that it would just be a matter of a few hours before we would run out of air and die. My father tried to reassure me; and as long as I could hold onto him, to feel his strength, somehow I thought we would survive this journey. The engine made a sudden start, and we fell all over each other. Our toilet consisted of one small pail for 40 people, and soon it smelled terribly.

After a while, I fell asleep, but was suddenly awakened by a jerking stop.

Outside we heard men yelling at each other in German..... we had arrived in Germany and a worse feeling came over me. We were hungry, scared and extremely cold. After a half hour when they had changed engines, we were on the move again. I now knew I was in the land of the enemy. Before, even though we were imprisoned, I was still in Holland, my home, but now it was different. After a few more hours, we stopped again, and again I was awakened. Through a small opening I could see it was getting light, and even though I didn't have a watch, I guessed it was about seven in the morning. I could see a large sign, "Bremen," a railroad station, but there wasn't much left of it. Someone told us it had been bombed the night before. It was a hopeful sight to see, a piece of Germany's soil destroyed. I wished they had bombed the railroad tracks as well, so we wouldn't have been able to get through. We remained there about an hour. In the meantime, we were all getting colder and colder, and so very hungry and thirsty. Those few who had been able to fall asleep started to wake up.

Three hours later, we came to another station, which turned out to be the end of our trip. For most of the men, women and children on this transport, it was to be the last time they ever saw this place. We had to wait for another half hour before the door was unsealed and opened, and had some time to get our things together, to wake up the sick people and help them. I approached one old man who appeared to be in a deep sleep. I shook his arm and body to wake him up, but.... he was dead. He was not the only one.... altogether we lost 4 children, six women and three men. I had never touched a dead person before. It is an experience that will remain with me forever, but it was something I was going to have to get used to. I was to see thousands die.

Eventually the door was pulled open and it was the first time in over twelve hours that we had some fresh air, something we really appreciated, as the smell in this small confined area from the people and the non-existent toilet facilities had become unbearable. The sun was shining, but not for us. Our welcoming committee of German soldiers with machine guns and bloodhounds was waiting for us.

The soldiers barked at us: "Raus, Raus, schnell, schnell" (Out, out, fast! fast!). My father, who knew German, went over to one of the guards and told him that several people had died on the trip. The guard ordered several prisoners to pick up the dead bodies and carry them on their shoulders to the camp. There was nothing to do but follow orders. My mother, who was too weak to walk, was thrown into a truck. As my father was carrying a dead man, it was up to me to carry "all" our possessions wrapped in a blanket. We left the station, lined up in rows of five, and I saw the sign, "Celle," which is a small town near Hannover in the northern part of Germany. While we walked through the streets, we saw many German soldiers and civilians staring and laughing at us. After a seemingly endless walk, totally exhausted, we reached the front gate of Bergen-Belsen. We still had to walk for another half hour, as this was a very large camp, divided into several smaller units, and our section was at the farthest end.

Bergen-Belsen was about six square miles, totally surrounded by double rows of electrified barbed wire, with watchtowers manned by guards with machine guns and flood lights every 100 yards. Entering the camp, we saw several three-story brick buildings, for the S.S. guards. There was also a bar, a large canteen, all provided for our captors. We also passed a beautiful, spacious private house outside the camp, which belonged to the camp commandant. Looking through the barbed wire of one of the camps we passed, were many men in uniform, not German uniforms... they were Russian prisoners of war. After another 15 minutes, we got to another gate, which was the beginning of one large camp, divided into several small ones. In one of those we saw a group of skinny men, their heads shaved, dressed in prison-style blue and white striped suits. We found out later that these were Polish political prisoners, some of them had been there for five years. There were rumors that there was an American prisoner of war compound, but we never saw it.

When we arrived at our section, we observed several buildings; a shoe factory, an ammunition and military supply compound, a kitchen, and a small building with a large smoke stack. We later found out this was a crematorium.

When we reached our side of the camp, I saw that we were not alone. We were to join Greek Jews who had been there for several months, and were soon introduced to one of them, Albala. The S.S. had put him in charge of our camp, as a Jewish commandant.

He was a short, stocky man, with a loud squeeky voice, who yelled most of the time, and wore knickers. He had a beautiful wife and a cute 2-year-old son. They came from Saloniki, and because of his position had a separate small house for him and his family, which included a 13-year-old girl, Esther Cohen, also from Saloniki, whose parents had been killed, and Albala had adopted. She kept house for them and was a babysitter for their little son. I liked her, and she became my girlfriend, even though I could not speak any Greek and she didn't know any Dutch. The other kids in the camp used to tease me about her. This family was given better food than us, so they looked much healthier than the other prisoners. The other inmates were very unhappy with Albala, and accused him of being a collaborator. After the war was over, I heard that he was hung at the railroad station by the prisoners.

Another one of our Greek leaders was named Beppo, a little feisty man with a beret, who was in charge of labor details.

On our arrival they marched us onto a large open field (appel platz), for roll call. I was hungry, cold and tired and about to drop. There were S.S. men around, but they didn't say a word, because everything was left to the Greeks in charge of us. We were told to line up in rows of ten so that we could be counted, and we stood there for about two hours. First, they read the list of us who had just arrived, and we were to answer when our names were called. That was to see if any of us had escaped, which was impossible. In the meantime, we were freezing. In front of us stood a large stone barrack, and in back were wooden ones. The men were told to go to the stone barrack, and the women and children under 12 to the wooden barracks.

In our stone barrack, #11, I found that there were 12 sections and a washroom in each. My father and I were assigned to section C, and when we entered, it was as dark as a basement, as no lighting was supplied. The beds were made of wood, three tiers high, and the mattresses were plain burlap bags filled with straw. There were about twenty sets of beds in each room, housing sixty men and boys over 12 years old. We had a small sink with a small window at the back. By the time my father and I got to our room, all the beds were taken, except for two, next to the bathroom. We had no choice. As there was no door on the bathroom, at night the smell was awful, but there was nothing we could do but tolerate it.

At six o'clock that night someone came to tell us to register immediately. At the registration building about 100 people were ahead of us. In the meantime, it had started raining. We hadn't anything to eat for 29 hours, and I was totally exhausted, to the point where I didn't really care what would happen to me, like a drunk in a daze.

Suddenly, my attention was drawn to a beautiful, large German staff car that had pulled up. Out stepped a huge man, with a dark mustache, dressed in a flashy S.S. uniform. He walked like a cow, and his face was the kind seen in gangster movies. He looked around for a few minutes, saw that everything was under control, got back into his car, and left. We had just seen the Commandant himself, S.S. Hauptsturmführer Josef Kramer, who was to become known as the "Beast of Belsen."

The registration barrack had five young Jewish girls who were sitting at tables with old typewriters. When it was our turn, we reported to one of these girls. She asked us questions, such as: our names, nationality, my father's profession, place of birth, what foreign languages we spoke, ages, where we were from, and if we were in good health. She then said we could return to our barrack. Instead of returning to our building, we went to the hospital barrack to visit my mother. The hospital was filthier than our barrack. When we got there, she was asleep, so we didn't disturb her. Then we went to our own beds and it felt good to lie down, even though it was on a straw bag. In the middle of the night I woke up from the stench from the bathroom, but soon fell asleep again....

The next morning I was awakened by the noise of people already up; it was about 6 A.M. About an hour later, two men brought in a large container, (gamelle) with black coffee. We stood in line to get ours, but it wasn't worth the wait, as it tasted bitter and cold. We were told to expect this "breakfast" every morning from now on. I then started to dream of hot chocolate, cheese and eggs. My mouth was watering at the memory.

After this "delicious" meal, a man got up and asked for our attention. He introduced himself as Mijnheer Winkelman, and told us he was assigned to be the barrack leader. He tried to pick up our spirits by saying that we probably wouldn't be there too long, as the war would be over soon, to make the best of it so that all of us would be able to return to our homes. This helped a bit but not much. We were still hungry, cold, and scared.

At nine o'clock we were told to line up outside the barracks. We waited there for an hour in the icy cold, typical Northern German winter weather. An S.S. man came and marched us to the same big open field where we had been the day before. It was only around the corner, but it was even colder there, because it was so open, with no protection from the wind. Men, women and children, as well as babies, all shaking from the cold, stood there. Hardly anyone had overcoats or winterclothing; and looking at the guards, well-fed and warm in their heavy overcoats, what torture it was for us! If this had been just for a short period of time and just for this one day, it would have been bearable; but no, this was every single day, every morning at nine o'clock, for hours. This was called "appel" (roll call).

We stood there, four hundred of us, in rows of five, so we could be counted. We were never allowed to move or sit down. If we had to go to the bathroom, that was just too bad, we just did it in our pants. Why did they find it necessary to count us every day? They wanted to know if everyone was still there (as if one could possibly escape). One could not try to escape without being electrocuted by the barbed wire or shot by a guard in the watch tower. Even if one had managed it, where could he go? He would be in the middle of Germany with no money, no food, obviously a typical underfed prisoner. He could hardly knock on someone's door and announce that he had just escaped from a concentration camp. "Would they please help him?" He would be picked up by the Gestapo before you could say: "Heil Hitler," and be shot on the spot. To make a comparison, it would be like jumping off a ship in the middle of the Pacific Ocean.

There were days of standing on the "appel plaats" from two to as long as ten hours. Usually some miscount occurred, and they would have to start all over again.

One brutally cold day, we had an exceptionally long appel. Someone was missing, so the Krauts counted and counted, but they could not come up with the right figure.... someone WAS missing. Then the "missing" person was found. About an hour before appel, a little four year old girl had died; and as was the order of the day, her body was thrown on top of a heap of others. Somehow, it had slipped UNDER that of an adult. This entire procedure took about eight hours, and by the time we were finally dismissed, about 100 people had fainted.

I was so frozen, I could barely move. I don't know how I made it, but I managed to drag myself to the hospital barrack to my mother. I crawled into her bed, and it was an hour before I thawed out enough to speak. Terrible thoughts were going through my mind, and I really didn't care what happened anymore. I felt we would never get out, as my mother was not getting better, my father was getting weaker from hard labor, malnutrition, beatings, humiliation, degradation and worst of all, hopelessness. People were dying all around me. The hunger pangs were driving me crazy; it was the lowest point of my life.... I turned to my mother, and very slowly, but quite determined, whispered to her, "Mommy, can't we please kill ourselves?"

My mother started to cry when she said, "Barry, I know what you are going through; after all, Mommy and Daddy and thousands of others are going through the same thing. I know it all looks very hopeless right now, and you have just gone through a very bad experience, standing there in the cold for so many hours. But I have a feeling, deep inside—I can't explain it—that we are going to get out of all this. Try to have hope, I am sure there is a future for us."

By this time I had warmed up a little, and her talk made me feel so much better. It gave me strength.

The Nazis called Bergen-Belsen a "privileged" camp, for these reasons: Families stayed in the same camp, although in separate barracks, and we could see each other every day. We were not tattooed, as they were in Auschwitz, Mauthauzen, and Buchenwald. There were no gas chambers. No, in this so-called "privileged" camp, they starved us to death, nice and slowly. When you are gassed, you die in a few minutes; but starvation can take weeks and months. Each day you feel the strength being sapped from you, you get thinner, turn blue, until finally you can't walk anymore. There were many people, mostly men, including my father, who were suffering from dysentery and edema, a condition where the body fills up with fluid, and the legs swell up as a result. All this, with the cold, the constant fear of being beaten, not to mention the lice and other diseases such as typhus and tuberculosis. These were not excuses for the Germans. Every day at six, all the men and women over the age of 16 had to perform slave labor.

Our food consisted of an inch-thick slice of black sour bread a day, and at noon we got a bowl of turnip water. Turnips were sliced into small cubes to be boiled in plain water. They took out the pieces of turnips, and we got the water that was left. This was our diet for one whole year, except for the times when we were penalized; in which case, we wouldn't get the slice of bread.

An extremely valuable commodity in our camp was salt. It was very difficult to get, but when we did, we put it on our slice of bread. We knew that salt was very important, and without it you would die. I saw many vicious fights among our people over a teaspoon of salt.

One day after appel, a list of 100 names was called off, and they were told to remain at appel after the others were dismissed. Our names were not on this list. I hung around to see why these people had been told to remain, because a good friend of mine, David S. was included. These were people whose foreign papers were not "in order," and they were being sent to Auschwitz. An S.S. officer appeared on the scene, and with the usual smirk, slowly walked around the group of frozen and frightened people. David was shivering from the cold and about to pass out, but I could do nothing for him. The S.S. man approached him and in an almost humane manner asked him, "Was ist denn los, kleiner?" (What is the matter, little one?) David answered him in half Dutch, half German, that he was very cold. The guard, smiling, as if he knew what David was going through, answered: "Don't worry about it, boy, in a few days you'll be in the ovens where it is nice and warm." That was my farewell look at a special friend.

Our section was divided into three parts separated by barbed wire. One was for the men, another for the women and children under 14, and still another for the two hospital barracks. Each had a gate and was locked at 8 P.M. We could see our mothers every day, if we didn't have to work. All those over fifteen were forced to work from six in the morning until ten at night. In the afternoon everyone came home to "eat" if indeed there was anything. This "lunch" break was twenty minutes, so there isn't much to do in such a short time. The turnip water was delivered to the camp in large containers, "gamellen," and held about 10 gallons. It took two men to carry these, then the barracks leaders would hand it out. Afterwards, all the boys my age had fights to see who would get to lick what was stuck to the inside walls. I would stick a hand into the container, all the way to the bottom and then go along the inside wall moving to the top, and if I hit it lucky, I got a tablespoon of this turnip water.

It was heartbreaking for me to see my dad coming home from his (slave) labor every night, totally exhausted, too tired to even talk to me. It hurt me deeply seeing him getting weaker, thinner, and more depressed every day. This strong, athletic, tower of a man was slowly but surely disintegrating before my eyes. I tried to think of the good old days in Amsterdam, when we used to go for walks in the woods, when he took me on the back of his bicycle, to Het Ijselmeer, go swimming, the days when people in our neighborhood treated him with respect and admiration. It was terrible for a son to see this happening to a father he loves so much.

One morning after my father and all the other men had left for work, a special appel was called. All boys between the ages thirteen and fifteen had to report to roll call. We couldn't get out of it, as the S.S. guards searched all the barracks to make sure we went. As I was fourteen, I was one of them. One thing we knew, it couldn't be good, it *never* was. We lined up in single file, and after an hour's wait, Commandant Kramer waddled onto the scene, accompanied by several of his henchmen as bodyguards. Whenever he came into our camp, he always came well-protected. I never figured out why he felt this was necessary. Was he honestly afraid he was going to be attacked by one of the prisoners, who could hardly get up and walk?

He announced the reason he had called us here was he needed some messenger boys. Walking along the long line of this sad-looking bunch, he would point at one of us and say: "Du, du" (you, you). That is all he said, but it was enough to take my daily freedom away. He came closer and closer, finally reached me, but passed. Suddenly he stopped. Was he coming back? He didn't seem satisfied with the amount or the type of boys he had chosen, so he did come back. I crossed my fingers and prayed that again he would pass me by, but this time I wasn't so lucky. He stopped in front of me and ordered one of his guards to take my name. I stood there, trembling with fear, as I had no idea what was going to happen.

Here I was, fourteen years old, in a concentration camp, hungry, cold, my mother seriously ill in the hospital, my father outside the camp performing slave labor with no hope of ever getting out or having any sort of future. I was scared to death, because during the past four years any new experience had been a bad one, and had made my life worse. I was content to spend the daylight hours hanging around with my friends; it was a routine, bad as it was. When something out of the ordinary happened, it was frightening, since I had no "human" rights. The guards could do as they wished; beat me, shoot me. Who was going to do anything about it? Who was there to protect me? Who would stand up for my rights? Up until four years ago, the people who were in charge of my life loved me. In the past four years my life was being controlled by people who hated me.

After they took my name, the Commandant departed after the usual "Heil Hitler" salutes from the guards. They told everyone to leave except for the boys who had been picked by Herr Kommandant. There were ten boys left. One of the high ranking S.S. men walked over to us and assigned us to our various posts. Some had to go to the entrance gate of our camp, some to other gates, a few to the main gate. I was assigned to inside camp duty. Whenever the commandant would come to our camp to inspect the barracks, I would have to walk ten feet behind him. If he wanted to enter a barrack, he would stop in front of it, I would then run ahead, open the door for him, and yell: "ACHTUNG!!" (Attention!). Everyone inside the barrack would then have to jump to attention. Secretly, I felt very important; here were all these people that had to stand up, just because *I* had yelled "achtung!"

Another one of my duties was to deliver special orders from the commandant to the barrack leaders all over our camp. They would then have to read it aloud to their people, sign the document to show that they had seen and relayed the order. Most of these messages consisted of various penalties; such as, no bread for three days, longer working hours, or no Sunday off. When I had shown these to all the barrack leaders, I was supposed to return them to the commandant's office, but on many occasions I didn't, and was never asked about them. The reason I wanted to keep them, was that I thought that these documents might be of some value, when the war was over. I kept them carefully in a small tin can I had hidden under my mattress.

One of the highlights of my days was when a message had to be delivered that was "urgent." One of the guards let me use his bicycle, so that I could go around faster, much to the envy of the other kids in the camp. They even accused me of "buttering up to the enemy" which, of course, was not true. I didn't mind this work, as at least the days went by faster because I had something to do. To be honest, it made me feel rather important, which I needed in this dreadful place.

Another advantage to this job was I was occasionally permitted outside our immediate camp, still within the larger camp, when I went to or from commandant Kramer's office. When I saw that the guards weren't paying much attention to me, as they got used to the idea of my walking around, I would sneak into the kitchen to find something to eat. After a while, I became adept at stealing without being seen. The people who were assigned to work in the kitchen were thoroughly searched every night to see if they had stolen any food, but they never suspected me. Sometimes I was able to walk out with quite a bit of bread stuffed into my knickers, but I had to walk very slowly. I would also get some salt, which was like gold. When I got back to our quarters, I would share these "valuables" with my parents. However, more often than not, my father would say that he wasn't hungry and tell us to eat.

Spring and summer came, which made life more bearable. Then more and more people were brought every week from countries such as: Hungary, France, Czechoslovakia, Austria, Italy; even from Morocco in Africa. I found these people fascinating, as they dressed differently from the rest of us. However, we didn't have enough room for these additional people. It came to the point that we were forced to put a fourth tier on top of the already three-tier high beds. As the ceilings were not very high, the top tier was about a foot down from the ceiling, making it almost impossible to get in or out. Many of them brought all kinds of diseases. The overcrowded conditions caused the spread of germs, and there were epidemics.

Another thing we had to live with was lice, one of the worst things we had to put up with. Once you got one louse on your body, there was no way of stopping them. They constantly lay eggs, and they multiply faster than rabbits. All you had to do was to touch a person with them, and within a few days you would be infested. People couldn't help touching others, as the camp was overcrowded. Your body, especially around the stomach and pubic area, begins to itch, you start scratching, and soon your body is one mass of sores and blood. At night we would sit around and pick them off our bodies, then cut them in half with our thumbnails. Once a month we were marched to the delousing and shower building, but that didn't help enough. It might kill the lice on your body, but they never could destroy the eggs. Within a short period of time, your body would again be covered by lice.

Each camp had its own kitchen; ours was located outside but none of us were allowed there. Only the people who had been assigned to work there. The Germans had picked out ten of the prettiest girls for the kitchen, with an S.S. man in charge. At the end of each day, before being allowed to leave, they were searched thoroughly; in fact, sometimes, they had to remove all their clothes, and were raped.

One beautiful seventeen year old girl, named Stella, worked there. Her husband was seriously ill in the hospital barrack, and had just had an operation to have one of his ribs removed. He was very weak, and the Jewish doctor feared he was going to die. Since Stella worked in the kitchen, she made an attempt to get some extra food to him. The S.S. man in charge would sit at his desk next to the bathroom wall. In front of his desk were a lot of mirrors, so that whenever someone went to the bathroom, he could see exactly what they were doing. On this particular morning, Stella went to the bathroom and while there, hid some pieces of meat, butter and sugar under her clothes.

She was seen by the man in charge, but he kept quiet until it was time for the girls to leave. He let everyone go, except Stella, whom he took into his office. He pulled out his gun and made her take off all her clothes. All the precious items she had hidden fell to the floor. He raped her, and then reported her to the commandant. A few days later her husband died, a man of thirty who had once been a physical education teacher at a university. Stella was sent to Auschwitz, because she had taken some food for her dying husband.

In Bergen-Belsen, we had many S.S. women guards, who, at times, were more sadistic than their male counterparts. One of these animals, a high-ranking guard, was the dreaded Irma Grese, an attractive "woman" in her early twenties. She had blond hair and icy blue eyes, the typical specimen of Hitler's image of the Aryan "master race." She would visit us almost every day, smiling at the sight of starving people. She dressed in culottes, which looked like a skirt, but were really pants; and always wore boots and carried a riding crop.

One morning, as she was taking her usual morning stroll through our camp, one of our girls, about seventeen, failed to get out of her way; at least not fast enough to suit Fraulein Grese. She became very angry, ordered the girl to stop immediately, remove all her clothes, and to stand by the barbed wire fence without moving for the next twenty-four hours. She was "kind" enough to alert the guard in the tower, so that the girl wouldn't be shot. It was a bitterly cold day, and got colder that night. The next morning when we woke up, we all walked over to where the girl had been left standing.... she had frozen to death.

Because of the cramped space in our barracks, anything that was not needed for everyday use by the inmates, such as suitcases, was stored in a large building about a mile outside our camp. Every three months or so, we would be allowed to go to this storage place. We were not allowed to receive packages here as we had been in Westerbork, which added to our daily diet there.

One afternoon an announcement was made for those people who wanted to go to the storage place to report to the appel field at three P.M. As I had nothing better to do, and knew we had put one little suitcase away after our arrival several months ago, I reported with about fifty other people. After a long, dreary and tiring walk to the storage building, we were told we could go in two at a time, and would have two minutes to take care of our business. When it was my turn, I went over to our suitcase and opened it. I could hardly believe my eys.... I found a two pound bag of sugar, and a package of salt. I felt as though I had found a treasure, because salt was like blood plasma and sugar was like pure gold, not only to eat, but it could be used to trade for other items. I felt like a millionaire. When I returned to the barracks, I immediately ran to my parents and showed them my discovery. Obviously, these items had been left over from some of the packages we had received in Westerbork and were totally forgotten. The next few days we felt rich, had a feast and felt a bit of strength return.

There was a large food packing house just outside of our camp, where tons of food were kept for the German soldiers. Five of our camp inmates had to work there every day, with German S.S. men in charge. One of these Jewish men had a type of friendship with one of the officers. This "friendship," meant he was not beaten by him, and once in a while they would have a half-way decent conversation. This soldier would talk to him about what was going on in the outside world. The worker, Sam, felt he could trust the soldier and asked him to do him a favor. He had written a letter and asked his "trusted friend" to mail it for him when he got to town. The guard gladly obliged. However, instead of mailing the letter as promised, he took it straight to Commandant Kramer, where the letter was opened. It revealed facts about life in the camp.

The next day, I carried around a special order to all the barrack leaders; and, of course, read it. Everyone, man, woman and child, sick or old had to report to the Appel Plaats that afternoon at four o'clock. Rumors had spread around the camp about the "letter incident," and we were all curious. I discussed it with the guard who had given me the order, and he confidentially told me that the Commandant was so angry about the letter, he was going to personally shoot the writer in front of the entire camp population.

As soon as I heard this, I went to Mr. Albala, our Jewish camp commandant, and told him. Albala immediately went to the guard at our gate, and asked for permission to talk with the Commandant and pleaded with the "Beast of Belsen" not to kill the man and give him another chance.

He succeeded, after talking to him for over an hour, into changing his mind, at least as far as shooting was concerned. Kramer felt that this incident should not go unpunished. We soon found out what he meant by that. He decided to punish EVERYONE in the camp with one of the severest penalties he could possibly give; he took our food away, no bread for three whole days. It doesn't sound like much, but in our condition, we couldn't afford to miss even *one* day of bread, as it would in reality be a death sentence for many of us on the brink of starvation. This was punishment for four thousand men, women and children. It would surely mean death for hundreds of them. We just didn't know what to do, and many began to panic.

Mrs. Rosenberg, one of our barrack leaders, knew Josef Kramer personally, as they had been schoolmates in Berlin before the war. I had seen them talk together for hours about old times. It dawned on me that this lady may be our last hope in trying to influence him. I suggested to Mr. Albala to ask Mrs. Rosenberg to go talk Kramer into changing his mind. He appealed to her and she consented. Albala accompanied her to the gate to ask one of the guards permission for Mrs. Rosenberg to talk to the Commandant. Officially, Albala was the only Jew in our camp permitted to talk to Germans, without being spoken to first. The guard's answer was a flat: "Nein!" (No!) He said perhaps when there would be another guard on duty, but he wasn't going to be the one to let her out. This news, which spread around like wildfire, came as a terrible shock to all of us.

I tried to figure out how to get through the next few days. What could I do to get my mind off food? Then I got an idea; there was a fellow in my barrack who had a chess set. I went over to him and asked him if he wanted to sell it to me. Of course, I couldn't buy it with money; there wasn't any, and money was useless here. I managed to talk him into selling me his chess set for two rations of bread, which meant that I wasn't to get bread for FIVE WHOLE DAYS. I had my reasons. I took the set to my bunk, and for the next three days I did nothing but play chess with my friend, Walter. We concentrated on the game so intensely that we forgot all about our hunger, so the days went by quickly. The other people weren't as fortunate as I. Forty people died of starvation in those three days, most of whom were men. It seemed that women were more capable for some unknown reason, of surviving such an ordeal.

The effects of those terrible three days were felt for a long time. So many more people died, that the Germans didn't even bother to take the dead bodies away. We had to pile them up beside the barracks, and once a week a large truck would come take them away. It was horrible to see all those dead, emaciated bodies there; sometimes the pile was six feet high. I would get sick to my stomach from the smell, but after a while, I somehow got used to it, or rather I HAD to, and tried to ignore it. It was dreadful to see bodies of family or friends just laying there such a long time, without a decent burial.

There were two eighteen year old boys, Frans and Pieter, who had been picked by the Commandant to live outside our camp, alone in a small hut behind the crematorium. No one ever had any contact with them, nor they with us. It was all very secret. We knew that they were assigned to burn the bodies of our dead, but what could possibly be the "big secret?" We heard that they received the same food the guards received, got cigarettes, and even heat in the winter.

On an errand outside our camp, I had a conversation with Pieter. We both carefully looked around to make sure that no one saw us talking, and he told me the sordid details of their job. When the dead bodies were brought to them, they were to remove all the gold teeth from the corpses, remove their shoes, eyeglasses and even their hair. They would then carefully pile these items outside in neat stacks. After burning the bodies, they would then remove all the bones, and put them outside. Once a week a truck from a nearby chemical plant would pick up the bones and make soap out of them. He told me that they could not possibly keep up with the ever-increasing amount of bodies that were brought to them for cremation. Even though he looked healthy and well-fed, I wouldn't have traded places with Pieter.

Our camp physician was an S.S. man, Dr. Fritz Klein, who was a graduate from Auschwitz. He looked like a kindly man, the way we like doctors to look, but just don't get caught in his clinic. His favorite word was: "Abschneiden" (cut it off). If you had a sore finger or toe, he'd cut it off; after all, that was more fun, and so much easier than treating it. I came under his "care" on several occasions for infected sores on my feet, but luckily he didn't cut off my foot. He would take a sharp knife and cut a large square around the sore, to remove the problem, instead of opening and simply draining the infected area.

Our other enemy was the weather. The Germans seemed to know exactly what they were doing when they built Belsen in Northern Germany. The winters were unbearably cold, and there never was much of a summer. If it wasn't snowing, or very windy, it was raining. It wasn't only the lack of food we had to cope with, the lice, the beatings; no, there was also the weather.

In May of 1944, a large transport of people, about a 1000, came to our camp, to add to our long list of dying. Where were they going to put them? We soon found the answer. In the middle of that night, we were all awakened and ordered to move to another barrack. It was raining heavily, which made the move even worse. When we arrived, we found that there were not enough bunks to go around. One of the guards then informed us that TWO people were to sleep in each bunk. As these beds were only three feet wide, imagine what it was like to sleep with someone else in such a small space. I slept that way for the next eight months. It was so crowded, that most of us didn't get a chance to wash anymore, causing even more disease. At night I could feel the rats walking over my face and body; this was something I was never able to get used to. There were men beside me, under me, over me and next to me, who died, more and more each day. They were beaten by the S.S. guards for no reason, but then they didn't need any.

I saw my father beaten and kicked by an S.S. guard who looked no older than seventeen. It was all I could do not to run over and kill him with my bare hands. When my dad came home that night, he fell on the bed and was unconscious for two hours. When he came to, all he could say was, "It isn't the physical pain that hurts, it is the mental pain, to be beaten until I drop by a seventeen year old boy without being able to do anything to defend myself." Then he fell asleep again, while I just sat there watching him. His whole body had swollen up like a balloon as a result of starvation. Many other men had died this way, and I sat up that whole night worrying, wondering if he would ever wake up again.

Rumors that Hitler's armies were suffering great losses at the Russian front were being confirmed by the fact that quite a few of our S.S. guards suddenly disappeared. We heard they had been sent to the Russian front. In their place we got old Werhmacht (regular army) men.

There were to be more surprises. As mentioned, there was another camp, part of Bergen-Belsen, that was for Polish political prisoners, and some of these men had been there for many years. Commandant Kramer personally picked three of these men, known for their open anti-Semitism and sadism, and offered them a great opportunity. If they promised him to "beat the hell out of those Goddamn Jews every day," he would send them to our camp, give them special living quarters with good food, heat, showers, and cigarettes. Naturally, they were eager to accept his offer. After a few weeks of fattening-up, they arrived, complete with rubber hoses, and promptly started to "carry out" their duties. They were called "capos," and were more barbaric and sadistic than the S.S. All day the capos walked around indiscriminately beating not only men, but women and children as well; usually around their heads, as this was much more effective. We had to take our caps off as soon as we saw one of them approach us. Prior to being let loose in our camp, Kramer's final instruction to them was: "Je mehr tote Juden Sie mir bringen, desto besser ist es!" (The more dead Jews you bring me, the better it is).

I witnessed one of these capos beat a young woman in her face with one of those rubber clubs until the blood streamed from her eyes, and half of her teeth were knocked out.

One day I was helping to move a little old lady who had to be hospitalized. She walked behind me while I carried her two large and one small suitcases. When I turned the corner of one of the barracks, I bumped into one of the capos who had been running. He almost knocked me over. He tore the suitcases from my hands and started to beat me with his rubber club on my legs and shoulders. He became so excited, that he dropped the club. He didn't pick it up, and continued by kicking me and hitting me with his fists. He kept this up for about three minutes, but that was more than enough; another minute and I would have fainted for the first time in my life. Thank God, he stopped, and before he left, he smiled at me and said, "That will teach you."

As I picked up the suitcases and continued my journey, I noticed a girl standing there who lived in my mother's barrack; in fact, she slept next to her. I made her promise not to tell my mother about what she had seen. I don't think Mom ever found out, for which I am glad; as she would not have taken this lying down, and would have shown her anger, and wound up the loser, as a result.

Greetje, a sixteen year old girl prisoner, had parents who had owned a restaurant in Amsterdam, where we would go in the good old days. She was as hungry as the rest of us, but found her own way to help herself and her mother with some food rations after her father had died.. One of the capos took a liking to her, and soon the two of them were having an affair. He would sneak into her barrack almost every night. She gave her body to him, and in return she received some bread and cheese. Everyone knew about it, as it was common knowledge. Some people didn't blame her for her actions; after all, when one is that hungry, unusual relationships are made. But there were many who accused her of consorting with an enemy, who was responsible for having beaten to death five or ten of her campmates that day. She eventually fell in love with her capo, and when the war was over managed to smuggle him into Holland to marry him. On their wedding day; on their way to the city hall for the ceremony, her husband-to-be, the ex-capo, was kidnapped, driven to the German border, and promptly hanged.

"If you move, I'll shoot!"

Last look at our home.

Westerbork: Entertaining our captors.

ROLL CALL

Meal Time

Daddy, will you ever wake up again?

Bergen-Belsen: Does anyone care?

"Mommy, can't we please kill ourselves?"

"Wollen Sie Wieder zurückgehen nach AMERIKA?"

RIJKSINSTITUUT VOOR
OORLOGSDOCUMENTATIE
NETHERLANDS STATE INSTITUTE FOR WAR DOCUMENTATION
INSTITUT NATIONAL NÉERLANDAIS POUR LA DOCUMENTATION DE GUERRE
NIEDERLÄNDISCHES STAATLICHES INSTITUT FÜR KRIEGSDOKUMENTATION

HERENGRACHT 474 - AMSTERDAM-C

Datum	Aantal gedeporteerden	Kamp
14- 9-1943	305	Theresienstadt
21- 9-1943	979	Auschwitz
19-10-1943	1007	"
15-11-1943	1149	"
16-11-1943	995	"
11- 1-1944	1037	Bergen-Belsen
18- 1-1944	870	Theresienstadt
25- 1-1944	949	Auschwitz
1- 2-1944	908	Bergen-Belsen
8- 2-1944	1015	Auschwitz
15- 2-1944	773	Bergen-Belsen
25- 2-1944	811	Theresienstadt
3- 3-1944	732	Auschwitz
15- 3-1944	210	Bergen-Belsen
23- 3-1944	599	Auschwitz
5- 4-1944	289	Theresienstadt
5- 4-1944	240	Auschwitz
5- 4-1944	101	Bergen-Belsen
19- 5-1944	453	Auschwitz
19- 5-1944	238	Bergen-Belsen

Listing of our transport from Westerbork
to Bergen-Belsen

```
751. S lk -J co i        Il e          8. 9.11   Angestellte
752. v Si s              Jc ef         23. 1.75. Kommissionär
753. v Si s-Sl p         Si a          26. 5.82  ohne
754. S lk                Hi olf        16. 2.40  ohne
755. S rl i              Ju la         18. 7.35  ohne
756. S r? i              Ji lith       7. 7.36   onne
757. S r  i              Sr uel        18. 7.35  onne
758. S r  i-T:           Ju ith        19.12.03  ohne
759. S r ni-D: t s       Si pora       15. 3.06  Angestellte
760. Sie c               Fe l          26. 1.24  Landarbeiter
761. i    l              Si ion        8. 5. 94  Kaufmann
762. i  etg              ur el-        14. 2.87  Kontorist
763. ii  n               Si gf ied     17. 3.86  Kaufmann
764. Si  n-S ot n        La ia ie      14. 5.95  ohne
765. Si  ne              Er ist        7. 8.19   Angestellter
766. Si s - ro k         An ia         28.10.19  Kontoristin
767. Si i s  n           Go sc lk      31. 6.79  ohne
768. Si a s n  t         Jo a          3. 5.96   Fabrikant
769. Si e s p 1-F se e c;(r  He ta     7. 4.06   ohne
770. Si n s p 1-G st n 1: Le           17. 1.73  ohne
771. Sl                  El as         29. 1.76  Diamantkaufmann
772. Sl -C mr as         Es her        15. 8.71  ohne
773. Sl  j               Ep raim       6. 5.82   Kaufmann
774.  p-v.d Y r          Vr uv je      17. 6.84  ohne
775. Sl n                Is de r       17.12.22  Tischler
776. Sno k               Ir ac         30. 6.77  ohne
777. nc k-F s            He nt e       24. 1.81  ohne
778. nc k- : Le u        Pa li e       4.11.81   ohne
779. oe                  J. ob         2. 7.22   Beamter
780. ot -1 m n           La et e       14. 5.20  Diamantarbeiter
781. or er e  g          Ka l          27. 2.04  Schuster
782. on s e  g t nk      K olie        27.11.04  ohne
783. eine n              Ha e Wolf     3. 3.30   onne
784. Spanjaard-Hoczeboom  Abigael      30.11.01  ohne
785. Spanjaard           Alfr         28. 7.03  Makler
786. Spanjaard           Harr         16. 5.29  ohne
787. Spe r- v ge         il :          18. 9.91  Beamtin
788. Spe r               Ma r. s       22.11.20  Kontorist
789. Spi er              Ar ol.        28.11.89  Kaufmann
790. pi er Schwe in      Ge da         21. 8.03  ohne
791. spi er              He nz         27. 3.32  ohne
792. wj g c              Ge ri         6.7. 66   Kaufmann
793. wan- cert je        Re he         1. 3.66   ohne
794. w rt        Je er as Xa xi x      6. 1.06   Diamantschleifer
795. w rt                Sa ue         10. 6.05  Schuhmacher
796. w rt-Dijk le        Ke ec e       6. 9.94   ohne
797. w                   J.ss eth      9. 2.30   ohne
798. w                   Mi je:        31. 1.39  ohne
799. c j                 Li tz         9. 9.26   Reparateur
800. S  a. t             Ju il a       17.12.66  ohne
```

Transport list to Bergen-Belsen, showing birthdate and occupation of my father, mother and me

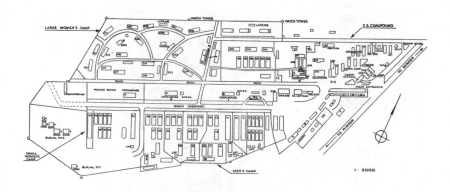

BERGEN-BELSEN CONCENTRATION CAMP

The Bergen-Belsen S.S. guards. Commandant Josef Kramer wearing long coat.

Bergen-Belsen's crematorium
Commandant Kramer is known to have said:
"The only way any Jew will ever leave this
camp, is through this chimney."

Irma Grese and Josef
Kramer after their arrest

Dr. Fritz Klein facing
a camp inmate accuser

One of the many mass graves

April, 1945 – S.S. women removing bodies under Canadian guard

Bergen-Belsen: women prisoners stripping the dead of their clothes.

XI. THE EMERGING AMERICAN

One unusually clear summer afternoon, while I was trying to catch up on some sleep, Mijnheer Winkelman, our
barrack leader, woke me and told me to go with him to pick
up our daily bread ration, as it was too heavy for him to
carry. I put on my worn-out shoes and went with him. The
weather was so beautiful, it was almost hard to believe
there was such a devastating war going on. The Germans
were practicing machine gun firing, as they did almost
daily. The windows were shaking, but we didn't pay much
attention as we were used to it. We reached the long tables
where the bread was spread out, and waited in line for our
rations. After five minutes, I heard a tremendous noise; I
recognized it as the sound of an airplane. I looked up, and
saw a plane headed almost straight for us at tremendous
speed. At first we thought it was going to crash on top of
us. Someone yelled: "Hit the ground!" which I did. The
plane began to fire for a minute; and just as quickly as it
appeared, it vanished. We were positive that some people in
the camp must have been hit. A few minutes later, the
plane returned again and started firing. It all happened so
fast, we almost didn't see it, but I did see the machine-
gunner in front of the plane. It had a double tail and glass
nose, with the big white star, which I recognized as
American. I was later told that this had been a P-38.

I got up from the ground and saw a huge fire outside our
camp. First, I ran over to see if my mother in the hospital

barrack was all right. I was worried about her, and she about me and my father, who was working outside the camp. She was safe, but the barrack next to her had been hit by bullets, and two women were wounded. One of them had been hanging some laundry on a clothesline, and got a bullet in her wrist. As I left my mother's barrack, I saw two men with a stretcher carrying a nurse who had also been wounded. She was taken to the camp operating room, which was very poorly equipped. The doctor tried to remove the bullet from her body, but she soon died. The woman who had been hit in the wrist died from loss of blood. On the way back to my own barrack, I saw about fifty Germans running with fire equipment, such as hoses, pails, and shovels. Two hours later, when all the men and women had returned from work, I found out what this had been all about.

There was a large building which looked exactly like one of our barracks, about a half mile outside of our camp, (still inside the larger camp), that was used for storing military supplies, rifles, helmets, gas masks, insulated boots, destined to be shipped to the Russian front that night. The Americans shot that barrack to pieces. We later found out that the entire building, complete with all its contents, was entirely demolished. How the Americans knew that this was the ONE barrack, identical to hundreds of others, to destroy, is something I never found out. In any case, it was a masterpiece of warfare. The Germans had used this barrack to store their military supplies, thinking that the "enemy" would NEVER bomb a place with thousands of prisoners.

I suspect there was a secret underground spy network located in Bergen-Belsen, perhaps even some of the German soldiers stationed there. Other than sadness about the two women who were unintentionally killed, we all felt wonderful about this incident, and prisoner morale was quite high for days. I again felt so proud to be an American; after all, hadn't *my* countrymen done this magnificent piece of work?

Most of the people in the camp were too weak to wash

themselves, and sanitary conditions left very much to be desired. Once a month, systematically to make sure they didn't skip anyone, we were marched to the delousing and shower building. This bathhouse was about a half hour's walk from our camp. We were never allowed to take these showers during the day, only at night. During the day, the German civilians in the vicinity of our camp, needed to use the water, and if we used it too, THEIR water pressure would be too low. The nights in that part of the country were bitterly cold, and it wasn't easy for babies and elderly people on these shower excursions. To make matters worse, the water was cold; and since there were only a few showers, ten people had to share one. We didn't get very clean this way, since most of us didn't have soap.

Upon entering this building, the first thing they made us do, was to strip naked, and put our clothes into bundles. While these were thrown into the delousing room, we were sprayed with white powder that was supposed to kill the body lice, but it wasn't very successful, and by the time we returned to the barracks, we were full of them again. During these sessions, it was nothing unusual for some of the guards to come in the shower room, and if they didn't like your face, they would kick you on your bare body with their heavy boots.

The guards whose faces I will never forget are Muller, a short, heavy man with a round face, and Herzog, who was in charge of plumbing. Prisoners, Bennie Bril, Dutch boxing champion, and Leo, a tall, handsome Greek worked for him, and they would go through the camp, fixing the plumbing. Herzog was an old guard who was in the Wehrmacht, the regular army, not in the S.S. He wore a ribbon on his uniform signifying that he had been to the Eastern (Russian) front, and as a reward, he was given the job as guard in our camp. We all called him "Popeye," as he had a protruding chin and was always smoking a pipe.

However, the worst of them all, was not a man, but a WOMAN. As mentioned before, her name was Irma Grese who, beneath that pretty appearance, had a heart of stone. She never touched anyone, but she delighted in tormenting us psychologically. Although she was very much adored by the male guards, she was the most feared and hated person by the inmates of Bergen-Belsen. We never knew what she was going to do next. For example, she came into our camp every day, eating big cheese sandwiches or an apple, purposely parading in front of us, as though to say: "Look what I have," in front of people who were starving to death.

One of her "games" involved me. One afternoon, while taking her daily stroll through our camp, this time with a large orange, she came in my direction. I tried to ignore her as well as her orange, but she knew I was one of the orderlies and commanded me to come to her. As we had been ordered by the commandant, I took off my cap, and stood at attention, five feet away from her. If I had stood any closer, she would have barked, "Zurück, zurück!!" (Back, back!!) They were afraid they would catch our diseases or lice (something we all had, thanks to them). She told me to go to all the barracks, gather all the boys between 13 and 15, and bring them to the big field within 15 minutes. This was some job, running to 29 barracks in such a short time. It took me 20 minutes to collect about 50 boys, who looked more like skeletons than children. She arrogantly walked around this group of shivering boys, as though she was the commandant, and picked ten of them including me, and dismissed the rest.

The ten of us were to follow her to the women's barracks, not knowing what she had in mind. She ordered all the women to gather their clothes in their blankets, bring a towel and soap, as they were going to the bathhouse. The boys were told to carry all their belongings, which I didn't mind, because I had been brought up to help ladies. When we arrived at the bathhouse, Fraulein Grese told us to go inside and help the women get undressed; not to make life easier for them but to embarrass all of us, especially the young boys. We had no choice but to follow her orders, and there was delight on her face as she watched this entire procedure. The next day, she did the reverse; she had the young girls in our camp go with the men: little innocent girls undressing old men.

148

Madame Grese drank heavily in the canteen with her fellow officers; and more often than not, she would come to our camp drunk. One morning, in this condition, she went to our administration building and wanted to know if any women had died during the previous night. She knew very well that some had died, not only during the night, but every hour of the day. She pointed to one name on the list and asked Albala in which barrack this dead woman was. She walked over there and told the leader to take her to that bunk. She ordered another woman to carry the body outside, follow her to the other side of the camp, dragging the body. Irma then ordered one of the capos to tie the two women together with some heavy rope she had brought for the occasion. Irma left, but soon returned with a can of gasoline. The woman who was alive began to scream, so Irma told the capo to hit her on the head with his club. She then poured gasoline over both women, lit a match and stood there watching, grinning, until the flames went out....

Frau Gertrud Slottke, whom we had the "pleasure" of meeting in Westerbork, decided to come and pay Bergen-Belsen a visit. Her mission this time was to see all the people with Palestinian passports. There were about 250 of them in our camp whom she interviewed. Two weeks later, all Palestinians were told to pack, and they left the next day. A few days later some people received mail from them from Turkey, saying that they were on their way to Palestine. The rumors were that they had been exchanged for military trucks (after the war, I heard that this had been true).

Because of this, my parents began to hope that maybe we too would some day be exchanged, and go to America. At this time my father told me that he was sorry that he had refused to speak English at home. He decided to give me English lessons, whenever he could find the time. He taught me the alphabet, how to count in English, and a few phrases, such as: "How are you?" "What time is it?" "How do you do?" "My name is..." "Thank you," "Don't mention it." I was very proud and excited, and told my friends that

"I could speak English." These lessons, unfortunately, didn't last long, as my father was getting weaker and weaker.

As time went on, during the second half of 1944, more and more people arrived from various other camps, supposedly to recuperate, and the food became more scarce. Every afternoon, after the "turnip soup" had been handed out, more and more boys would hang around to lick out the cans, and every afternoon there would be bloody fist fights. With all these new arrivals, we had about 35 different nationalities and we heard 10 or 20 different languages. Among these arrivals were about 75 French women and children, whose husbands and fathers were prisoners of war of the Germans.

On June 6th, 1944, I was at my usual post at the camp gate, when I overheard two guards talking to each other. One said, "Der Einfall ist eine Tatsache." Not knowing exactly what this meant, but seeing the worried looks, I figured it must be something important. I memorized their words. When relieved from duty, I ran to my father, and he said that it meant: "The invasion is a fact." They must have been worried about it, as the next day I had to take the following message around: "In case any enemy soldiers-(American or British) land in or near the camp, if anyone is caught trying to help them, the German guards are ordered to shoot you without warning." They began to dig foxholes around the camp and near the watch towers.

One of the men in our camp managed to get a German newspaper, and he read us the news about the invasion. It had taken place in France instead of Holland, as so many people, including the Germans, had expected. The day after D-Day, we had an air raid. There were many planes flying so low, I was sure they were going to land right in our camp. Some of them were shot down not far from us. It was a sorry sight to see the flyers bail out, because we knew all too well what was waiting for them. As soon as they landed, if they were not shot first, they too would be captured and sent to a prison camp.

In October of 1944, we heard from some new arrivals that

Holland had been invaded by the Allies, were well on their way to Germany and Berlin, but the Nazis had managed to defeat them. This had occurred near the Dutch city of Arnheim where the entire invasion plot in Holland had been sabotaged by Dutch Nazi sympathizers. We were all extremely depressed and disappointed when we heard this news, but the Germans were so happy, they wanted to celebrate. That night, every inmate above the age of eighteen got ten cigarettes. The tobacco was "ersatz" and they tasted bad, but most people enjoyed smoking them anyway, as it took their minds off their hunger for a while. The Germans gave each of the children under eighteen a quart of milk. It was mostly water, but it was a good feeling to taste milk again.

It's hard to believe there was entertainment in this place, but some people somehow managed to provide some. A young Dutchman, Jackie Goudsmidt, who looked like Clark Gable, played the violin very well. On Sunday afternoons, he would stand outside our barrack, weather permitting, and play for us.

My mother gave talks in the hospital about America. The people were totally fascinated with her descriptions of life in New York City. She had a wonderful gift of expression, which later helped her to make a living. These stories took people out of their misery for a while. I hung onto every word like a sponge, soaking up as much as possible about that paradise, so many miles away, America. After all, it was MY country she was talking about. It was like going to a movie, as I could actually see the tall buildings, the Statue of Liberty, the many restaurants, theatres, Central Park, the George Washington Bridge, Coney Island, Radio City Music Hall, the Empire State Building, and the world's largest department store, Macy's where my mother had worked. How she loved America.... and longed to go back some day, and was so proud she had given birth to an American.

In the "old days," she had been in the choir at "Het Concertgebouw" in Amsterdam under the direction of Willem Mengelberg, because she sang well. When she was feeling a little better, she would give a rendition of "Ramona," one of her favorite songs, and at the end, people would break out in thunderous applause; she enjoyed all this attention.

There were also people who had been to such places as Palestine and other interesting countries who gave talks. In this way we learned something about our neighbors and the world.

One Sunday afternoon, during a concert, one of the guards suddenly burst in, walked over to the musicians, and took their instruments away. They were quite valuable, but were never returned. One thing they could never take away from us; no matter how hard they tried, was our knowledge, unless they killed us. We had professors and doctors who gave lectures on various subjects, but *my* favorite speaker was my mother.

After D-Day, in clear weather, we had air alarms every day. It was nothing unusual to see hundreds of planes fly over, but since the invasion, the Germans thought they might land. Sometimes the sky was so clear, we could actually see the planes drop their bombs, probably in Hannover. Whenever this happened, we felt great knowing that some part of Germany was being destroyed, and it was bringing us that much closer to the end of the war. It was such hope which could, in spite of our condition, keep us going for a while.

One time we didn't enjoy the bombing. The English one night hit the factory in Hannover where our bread was made. This meant disaster for us; we didn't get ANY bread for four days. During that time 150 people died, four people were driven to insanity, and ran to the barbed-wire fence to be shot or electrocuted. The remainder turned from humans to animals. Everyone was in the way, cranky; and worst of all, the people began to steal food from one another. They just couldn't help it. Some had been fortunate enough to save some bread for such times, and hid it under their mattresses or rolled it up in their blankets, as there was no other place to hide these "treasures." When others found it and took it away, there were many fights. There had to be some solution; we just couldn't go on like this. A court was formed with the permission of camp commandant Kramer.

A German Jewish judge and a lawyer were appointed. When someone was caught stealing, a trial was set up in court, which was nothing more than a table and a few chairs outside, where everyone in the camp could observe. Kramer came and enjoyed watching one Jew punish another. The commandant gave the judge permission to use a dark cellar outside the camp as a jail for those who were found guilty. Of course, it wasn't pleasant for one prisoner to punish another, but it had to be done. People who stole bread were dangerous. Even if they had taken one or two slices it could mean death for the victim. These trials took place once a week, and usually someone would end up in that cellar, even though he or she had a defense lawyer.

Every afternoon, after the men and women had returned to their work from the lunch break, one of the guards came for me to bring the prisoner in the cellar his food, which consisted of bread and water. A man who had been sentenced to 65 days, and had served 41 of them, was dead when I came to bring him his food. These cellars were small, about 5 to 6 feet, very damp, cold and dark, with just a few pieces of straw on the floor. This punishment was responsible for at least some people managing not to steal, and it did slow down a bit.

However, such was not the case with one 11-year-old boy in my barrack. His name was Hans Slachter.

Hans, suffering from terrible hunger, as we all were, could not control himself, and stole whatever he could find from people around him. His father was working in the shoe factory 16 hours a day, so he saw very little of him, and the boy was alone the entire day. He would wait until most of the people either had gone to work or outside. Remaining in the barrack alone, he used the excuse that he wasn't feeling well. One day he was caught taking a piece of bread from under the mattress of the bed next to him, was reported to our barrack leader, who had a long, stern talk with him. Hans promised he would "never do it again," but a few days later, he was caught stealing again. This time he was told that his father would have to be told about this. When his father returned from work that evening, the barrack leader told him what had happened. Even though totally exhausted, his father took Hans over his knee, in front of us all, and beat him. Hans started to cry, and between his sobs, promised again this would never happen again. Everything seemed right for a while, but then he was caught again stealing bread. Very angry this time, the barrack leader told him he had no choice but to turn him over to our "court."

Two days later trial was held, and it was decided that Hans needed supervision. An old man in our barrack, too old to work, was appointed as his guardian. For awhile things went very smoothly. Hans and his guardian formed a warm friendship; he looked upon this old man as his grandfather, and the old man saw in this boy his own grandson, who had been shipped to Auschwitz. One morning when Hans went to his new grandfather's bunk to wake him, the man was dead.... A new guardian was appointed, a man who had been a schoolteacher in Holland, and they also got along famously. Three weeks later this man was transported to Auschwitz. Hans felt totally lost and abandoned, and returned to his old habit of stealing. Again his father punished him, but two days later he did not have to worry about his son stealing anymore.... Little Hans had died in his sleep....

During the summer and fall of 1944, several transports, consisting of women and children only, arrived in our camp from Auschwitz. From these women we heard two startling things. One, the reason they had been moved from Auschwitz to Bergen-Belsen was that the Russians were moving into Nazi-occupied Poland. The Germans, for some reason, didn't want "their" Jews to fall into the hands of the Russians, so they moved them West. The other unbelievable news was that the Germans were killing thousands of Jews every day in gas chambers and ovens.

We had thought that Jews who were sent to Poland had

to perform slave labor, as we did in our camp. The Germans had very carefully planned to keep this a big secret, because if this had become known, people certainly would NOT have calmly walked to their deaths without putting up a struggle. The Germans would have had quite a problem on their hands, which would have prevented them from systematically killing 6 million people. They told us that when people arrived at Auschwitz, they were first divided into two groups: 1. Young, healthy men and women between the ages of 18 and 35, who could perform slave labor. 2. Children and people over 35 who were totally useless to the Nazis. This group was told to take off their clothes, line up outside a large building to "take a shower." No one suspected anything, since the Germans had even arranged for an orchestra to play for them as they were waiting in line for the "shower", to keep them calm. Once inside this "shower" building, the doors were locked, and instead of water, lethal gas came out. The guards watched through a window to see when the last person had stopped struggling or screaming, and they were all dead; then the bodies were removed to the crematorium. The Germans had seen to it that there was absolutely NO contact between the regular prisoners and those who were assigned to carry out this "mission." The actual killings were done in a camp called Birkenau, some distance from Auschwitz.

We found this extremely hard to believe; but all the women who had come from there assured us that it was true.

With these women, came many children, most of them young girls, and we soon got to know some of them. Many of them had come from foreign countries, and we couldn't talk to each other. There were several Dutch girls, and we used to play together. It wasn't until a few years later that I found out that one of these girls had been Anne Frank....

Some news managed to come through, how, I don't know. Perhaps one of the guards, feeling the end of the war was coming confided in one of our group. When you want something to happen, and are in the situation we were, you start grasping at straws; when we got some news, we would talk about it all day. By the way the German guards were acting, we knew the Americans were getting closer. They started to take it out on us. Every day all the men were beaten, some with big clubs, some with bare fists, and some were kicked by heavy boots. As they were so weak, many of them fainted, some never to get up again.

I could see my dad getting weaker and thinner. When I saw him give my mother his share of bread, I knew he had been depriving himself of food to keep us alive. He would offer me some bread too, and when I refused to take it because he needed it himself, he would tell me that he had managed to get some "extra." I then knew he was giving up his life for us. Soon, he too was hospitalized, totally exhausted and unable to move without help. The hospital "care" didn't help him as there was no medicine. Patients would just lie there until they died...

One night I was assigned to take a message to my father's hospital barrack, and took advantage of the opportunity to visit him to see how he was. He looked terrible, lying in a dark corner in a dirty bed. Then my eyes fell on a man who was brought in from work by some others. His clothes were full of blood and he was unconscious. The doctor came over to discover what had happened. My dad told me to leave, as he didn't want me to see this, saying, "These things happen every day, and I am getting used to it. I just turn my head the other way, and make believe nothing is going on." As I was saying goodbye to him, telling him to get as much sleep as possible, I overheard the conversation between the doctor and the men who had brought in the injured man. A guard had come over to him while he was digging a foxhole, and began to beat him, first with his fists and boots, and then with his rifle butt on his face. I looked at the man's face, what was left of it, and saw blood coming out of his eyes, nose and mouth. The next day when I went back to see my father again, I asked him about him. My dad told me that before the doctor was able to do anything for him, he died. One of so many men who were beaten to death.

My father, only 39 years old at this time, who had been

an athlete, was reduced to a shell of a man. The Germans had managed to sap all his energy, health, and dignity. He was with all the other unfortunate men, who could not get out of bed, totally helpless, just waiting for death to take them. In spite of the fact that physically all there was left of him was skin and bones, his mental capacities were not affected. In that dark corner, with absolutely nothing to do all day but think of his hunger, he found a way to occupy himself; he wrote hundreds of recipes on toilet paper. He also prepared a diet of light food, for the time of liberation, so our bodies could gradually get used to good food again. He said it would take about six weeks before our bodies would adjust to normal food.

My mother, on the other hand, would constantly keep swallowing, as though she were eating. She would fantasize about steak, potatoes, vegetables, and actually think she was swallowing the food. I was thankful that I didn't have time to think about these things, as I had to work all day, but the thought of both my parents in the hospital, dying of hunger was always on my mind.

Leaving Bergen-Belsen carrying 65 pounds of love

XII.   RECIPE: ONE PART JOY—
ONE PART GRIEF

January 21st, 1945, started like most of the other miserable winter days. I woke up at six in the morning, had some breakfast of black muddy water, tried to wash, saw the men in my barrack leave for work, and at nine o'clock went to the daily appel. This time it only took one hour, as at the first count all were present and accounted for. After appel there was nothing to do but wait for twelve o'clock, when they would bring us our usual lunch, turnip water. This day was not to end like all the other days, the 655 days since we were first imprisoned.

An hour after roll call, a German guard came to my mother's barrack and informed her, rather politely, that Herr Commandant Kramer wanted to see her, her husband and her son, in his office immediately. She became frightened, as she knew from other past experiences with others, that if you were called to his office, it was not good. It usually meant deportation to the Auschwitz extermination camp. My mother got dressed, and asked one of the ladies in her barrack to tell me to come right away. As my father was much too ill to move, she did not tell him about this. I got to my mother's barrack, and we went to Kramer's office. We were surprised, to say the least, that when we approached the gate of our camp, the guard immediately opened it, without questioning us first. He must have known something we didn't.

After a half hour's walk through the snow and wind, we arrived at "my employer's" office. We knocked on his door, and immediately heard the answer: "Herein, bitte" (come in, please). He was sitting behind his big desk, with a cigar stuck in his ugly face. He didn't look up, and my mother and I just stood there waiting, literally shaking with fear. After what seemed like an hour, but was about a minute, he looked up   and asked: "Wo ist ihr Mann?" (where is your husband?).

My mother did some quick thinking. She couldn't tell him that he was in the hospital and too weak to walk, as she knew from the past that whenever there was a "good" transport, such as the one to Palestine, the participants were first given a physical exam. Anyone found not to be in condition to travel was scratched from the list. So my mother told Kramer, looking him straight in his eyes, that my dad was on a work detail outside the camp, and we were unable to reach him. At the time I didn't understand why she had told him this, as I knew what could happen to us if we were caught in a lie. I started to say something, as my German was better than my mother's, but she gave me a swift kick to shut me up. It turned out to be a brilliant maneuver on her part; in spite of her emaciated condition, she was capable of doing some quick-thinking on her feet.

"Wollen Sie wieder zurückgehen nach Amerika?" Do we want to go back to America???? We couldn't believe our ears! We thought he was up to one of his infamous tricks. My mother got her wits together and said; "Jawohl Herr Kommandant, eines Tages, das wird wunderbar sein" (Yes, Mr. commandant, one day that would be wonderful). He didn't appear to like this answer, because he snapped back, in German: "Well you don't have to, you can stay here if you want to, and die with the others. You dirty Jews are all alike, you are NEVER satisfied!" By now my mother realized that he might be serious, unreal as it seemed, and she said: "Oh please, Mr. Kramer, if it is within your power to return us to America, please do so!" He then got up, walked around the desk, stood in front of us and yelled: "Dann machen Sie sich bereit inn 10 minuten!" (then get

160

ready to leave in 10 minutes).

We ran from his office. Mom told me to go to my barrack and pack, as she was going to Dad to tell him; but I wanted to see his face when he heard this almost unbelievably good news. A guard was with us, who instructed Mom to write a letter to our family in America to expect us in the near future. This gave us additional reassurance that it was true. When we got to my father's barrack, the nurse at first wouldn't let us in, as it wasn't visiting hours. When we explained why, she was more than happy to permit it. My mother, very slowly, very carefully and calmly, told Dad what was happening. The expression on his sallow face barely changed. She said: "Freddie, let the spirit of knowing we are going to be free soon, make you get out of bed and give you the strength to make this trip." He said he would try, assuring us, "there really isn't anything wrong with me." We all knew how weak he really was.

I don't know how we managed it, but we got Dad dressed, wrapped our meager belongings in an old blanket, wrote a short note to one of my aunts in Brooklyn, New York, U.S.A., and said goodbye to a few close friends, giving them some things we wouldn't need any longer. Then we dragged ourselves back to Kramer's office, with me holding our possessions on one arm, and holding my father with the other. We were instructed to go to the bathhouse to be deloused. When we reached there, guards were waiting to search our things.

Now I became very nervous, as hidden in my blanket was my little tin can, stuffed with the official papers I had never returned to the commandant's office. I felt that now, with us going to the U.S., these documents might be of great interest. The S.S. man was going to search everything and would surely find them. What would he do to me when he did find them? Would he beat me? Would he order me to return to the camp? The tension was almost more than I could stand. He told me to unroll my blanket, and out fell my little tin can, right onto the floor. He looked down, and said: "Was ist denn das?" I didn't know what to say, so I mumbled, "Just some worthless souvenirs." He picked up the can, placed it on the table next to him and said: "Du kannst dass nicht mittnehmen." (You can't take that with you). I was relieved that he didn't open it, at least not while I was there.

After we were "deloused" and had taken a shower, we were told to walk to the exit of the camp, where a truck was waiting for us. Another half hour's walk, by this time my father was totally exhausted, as he hadn't walked in over three months. I carried him all the way; and although he weighed only 65 pounds, it was a heavy burden. I don't know how we we did it, but we finally reached the exit. As we walked outside the barbed wire and entered the truck, I thought, "Thank God for letting us see this place again." I had felt we would never leave Bergen-Belsen alive. In front of us was freedom, and behind us was a hell hole.

We drove through heavy snow for two hours to the railroad station in Celle, where we had arrived 10 days less than one year before. I thought I would never see it again, and realized then that my mother was right that day when I had given up hope and asked if we could kill ourselves, when she had reassured me that some day this would all be over. When we reached the station, we found a beautiful Red Cross passenger train waiting for us. We couldn't believe it, after having been transported in cattle cars. There were other people on the train, but we didn't know who they were. They were obviously not Jewish, as they were not wearing the big yellow Jewish star on their clothes, and they looked well-fed. The train had large red crosses on the side and top, as they didn't want the Allies to bomb it.

For the first time in years we felt heat and a nice tingling came over us; there were lights too; it was a wonderful feeling to sit on nice soft seats, instead of hard benches. I felt as if we were in Paradise. The train then started, and after we had been on our way for about a half hour, who entered our compartment, but our old "travel agent," Fraulein Slottke. She appeared to have changed into another person, and she even had a smile on that face when she told us, "You are now on a special exchange trip to

162

Switzerland. Here is a pair of scissors to remove your stars." I had been ordered to wear a star since arriving in Westerbork. When she handed me the scissors, temptation to do something else with them almost got the better of me. My mother read my mind, gave me a stern look, took the scissors from my hand and removed our yellow stars.

Fraulein Slottke continued, "Is everything all right? Are you satisfied?" We could not believe we were hearing such kind words coming from her mouth. Later, a German soldier entered our compartment and gave us cheese, butter, and THREE WHOLE ΄LOAVES of bread. We felt like royalty; we hadn't been that rich for over four years. We had a feast and ate like animals in a zoo. I devoured an entire loaf of bread myself, but soon found out that my stomach wasn't ready for it, because I got painful cramps, as if I had swallowed a dose of lye. It lasted for about three hours, and then the burning feelings went away.

When night began to fall, another soldier came in and gave us each a bowl of soup, but this time it wasn't turnip water; no, it was REAL soup, with *real* vegetables and *real* meat in it. Oh, I will never forget that first taste of something good and hot. After that, I ate some more bread, even though I knew I might get another stomachache, but I couldn't help myself, I just had to have some more. In the meantime, my father wasn't doing well at all, as he had eaten a lot of bread as well. Though it was the same sour black bread we had in the camp, it was much better because we had butter and cheese to go with it. It was too much too soon for him, even though he knew better; but he too couldn't help himself, and lost all self-control. As a result, he got dysentery, and had to go to the bathroom every four or five minutes. There were no doctors or nurses on the train, but someone gave him some black, charcoal-type powder, and told him to take it, but it didn't help. It was pitiful to watch him shuffle through the train hallway to get to the bathroom. He looked so skinny, but his legs were swollen. This new-found diet seemed to make me stronger, but had an adverse affect on my dad.

We three fell asleep, my father across one entire seat

meant for four people, and my mother and I sharing the seat across from him. When we awoke the next morning, the train was stopped at a large railroad station, in the city of Hannover. I would have given anything to be able to leave the train and walk around the city for a while, free, but no one was permitted off the train. I saw many bombed-out buildings. The Americans had done their job well, and there wasn't much left of them. To us it was a wonderful sight. I know it sounds blood-thirsty; but the more damaged German cities we saw, the better we felt.

Our next stop was Berlin where they brought us some breakfast. It was much more than we got during the past two years; a loaf of bread, butter, and some jelly. I was thrilled to receive all that food, but when I remembered the burning in my stomach I had the day before, I controlled myself and took it easy. I looked out the window, and for the first time in two years I saw real city life again, the first civilians I had seen, and found it interesting. Most of them looked depressed and poorly dressed, but compared to us, they looked very well. I could see that the streetcars were still running. It was the only means of transportation that the German civilians had for over six years, as there was no gasoline for private cars. The streetcars pulled a wood-burning oven behind them, and this was their fuel. The only cars I saw were official army cars, no bicycles, as there was no rubber for tires. The houses along the railroad tracks in Berlin had also been destroyed by Allied bombardments, even the station had been heavily damaged. There were many soldiers and officers in uniform. In Germany all military men carried rifles, bayonets and revolvers at all times, even off-duty. Later, I was to notice the difference in America.

On the other side of our platform, a long train of cattle-cars pulled into the station, and many people got out. I thought this was a usual Jewish transport, because who else would travel in cattle cars? But I was wrong. These were all German women and children who had been evac-uated from nearby farms.

Another train pulled into the station, and the passengers

walked into our train. They all were well-dressed and looked well fed, some even were fat.

We finally pulled out of the station in Berlin. As I walked through the train, I met a young girl my age, and we talked for about three hours. The entire conversation was in German, which I had learned during my stay in the camps. She was part of the well-dressed group that had just boarded. She told me she had lived in Berlin all her life, that her father was a Mexican citizen; at least he had Mexican papers and was an opera singer. She had three brothers, all of whom were "forced" to join the Hitler Youth; otherwise, their father would not have been allowed to work. Now they were on their way to Mexico on the same exchange trip with us. I became curious about the other people, about 100 of them. They had American and English cigarettes. How they got them, I didn't know. They were Polish and German, but seemed to have South American passports. I began to wonder why the Germans let all these people out of Germany. In about three weeks, I would find out.

After we pulled out of the Berlin railroad station, we didn't stop until we reached the German-Swiss border. We passed through many cities and towns, or rather what was left of them. Since it was the middle of the winter, the countryside was very beautiful, with snowy mountains. Some of the cities we passed through were Dresden, Schwein-furt, Stuttgart and Friedrichshaven. All of them were badly damaged, especially Friedrichshaven, which had been one of Germany's biggest industrial centers. Nothing was left of it, not one building was left standing.

Then we reached Konstanz, a city right on the border of Switzerland, but still in Germany. It was a very large station, and we had to wait there for about twelve hours, as we had many papers to sign. First, some German officials in civilian clothes came to all of us and handed us a card. It said: "I, the undersigned, do solemnly swear, that I will never pick up any weapons against the Germans, nor help to produce them in factories." After we had signed this, we were given another, which was very important. It was the official paper from the headquarters in Berlin, stating that we were now about to be handed over to the American authorities. Were we glad to see that! My father and mother were so happy, they started to cry, as they signed it.

Then the Grune Polizei came to visit us one more time. This time it wasn't to take us away from our home and throw us into a concentration camp. They came to search us from head to toe to see if we were trying to sneak weapons out of Germany. Everything seemed to be in order, but we still had to wait, something we were used to. We were on edge; we never knew what could or might still go wrong, and the whole thing would be called off.

Since I didn't have anything else to do, I walked around the train and met some more people who had come on the train in Berlin. They were Jews who had been in Vittel, the internment camp in France; and they looked very well, compared to us. We knew some of them as they had lived in Amsterdam, before being interned. They told me that they had received good food, and had received many Red Cross packages. They were wonderful to us; and gave me some chewing gum and my parents some real American cigarettes. I was in heaven, chewing and blowing bubbles. I had not forgotten how. There were about 50 of these Americans, just like me, except that they had been fortunate enough to possess American passports.

The nicest things they gave us were little paper American flags to pin on our clothes, and I wasted no time in doing so. I felt so proud wearing it that I went to the doorway of the train, which was open, where I saw a lot of Hitler Youth boys standing around. They saw my American flag, and I could see their faces were full of hate. I stuck my tongue out at them, knowing full well there was nothing they could do about it.

It then became dark, and we were still standing in the station of Konstanz. When I looked out the door, I saw a large swastika flag on one end of the station, and a large American flag on the other. Then some German Red Cross nurses boarded our train. They had come to get the sick people off. My father had become seriously ill and was barely holding on; he not only couldn't walk anymore, he hardly said a word and was in a semi-conscious state.... When the nurses came to our compartment and asked if anyone was ill, my mother, afraid that they would keep him in Germany because of his condition, told the nurses that everything was fine, that my father was sleeping.

Now the big moment had arrived, the official exchange was to begin. We lined up in front of the train, my mother and I holding up my dad between us. We were still on the German side, and on the Swiss side of the station, I saw German soldiers in uniform. Then the German authorities started to count us very carefully and slowly. We were then told to walk over to the other end of the platform, the Swiss side. This was the moment we had been waiting for for all these years. As we walked OUT of Germany into Switzerland, the German soldiers walked INTO Germany. I noticed as they passed us, that there were many more of them than there were of us. We found out later, that an agreement had been made between the German government and the governments of several North and South American countries, that the exchanges were to consist of FIVE German prisoners of war for one American. Now I knew why we had not been sent to the extermination camp. I was valuable property to the Germans. I remember thinking: "Not bad, here I am, just a fifteen year old kid, and I am worth five German officers."

It was unbelievable.... we were in Switzerland, a country NOT at war.... we were free! It was at this point that my mother began to realize that we were actually on our way to America. My father was in no condition to realize what was going on. I was thinking about all the excitement of the moment.

As soon as we had walked into Switzerland, we boarded another train, and slowly moved up about fifty yards, in order to get the entire train into Switzerland, safely away from the German border. My mother was trying desperately to tell my father and make him understand that we had finally arrived in Switzerland, that we were FREE. A group of Swiss soldiers and Red Cross nurses came aboard the train, bringing us some delicious hot soup and lots of kindness. I couldn't believe it. It was too much for me; I started to cry, and asked my mother, "Are there really good people left in this world?" She said, "Yes, there really are, and you just had an example of it right here, and from now on you will meet many more good people." I felt so happy, that I thought I was dreaming and afraid I would wake up and this wonderful dream would be over, and I would be back in my barrack in Bergen-Belsen. Then we got apples and all sorts of nice things from the Red Cross. Some Swiss soldiers came over to us and reassured us that we were free now, and didn't have anything to worry about anymore.

However, my mother was concerned about my father, and she asked one of the soldiers if he could possibly get a doctor for him, as it was very urgent. He immediately left the train as soon as we arrived in the town of Kreuzlingen. From the train window I could see the soldier enter a telephone booth. He came back and told my mother that he would return shortly with a doctor. Within a short time, a doctor arrived with two nurses. He took one look at my dad, and without asking questions, could see his condition. Even though he was in bad shape, we were not overly alarmed. We had seen hundreds of sick men in the past year, and felt that with the proper medical attention, he would be well in a few days. The doctor told my mother that he was going to phone for an ambulance, and send my dad to a local hospital. He assured us that my dad would get good care and would soon be all right. He was finally going to be in a real hospital with modern up-to-date medicines with people who cared. About five minutes later, two men dressed in white came with a stretcher. They carefully lifted my dad onto it. Mother and I kissed him goodbye, and told him that he was going to be fine in about two weeks, and would then be able to join us on our trip to America. I walked with the stretcher to the door of the train, kissed him again, and watched the men put my father into the waiting ambulance....

We remained in the Kreutzlingen station for about five

hours, and after midnight the train started moving. The sky was dark, but the houses were well-lit. It was a wonderful sight to see lighted buildings again, as we hadn't seen any for almost five years. Then I fell asleep.

The train came to a sudden stop and woke me up. We were in a city called St. Gallen, about 75 miles from the German border and about 70 miles from the hospital where my father was. We were told to leave the train. It was 7 o'clock in the morning, the snow was two feet high, but it wasn't cold. It was January 25th, 1945. For the first time in two years, I walked in a real town, and found it interesting after being away from civilization for so long. The civilians seemed so well-dressed and well-fed

A Swiss Army officer told us to board streetcars which were waiting for us. We rode through the center of St. Gallen and then to the outskirts, an interesting and enjoyable ride. After an hour, we stopped in the middle of the countryside, completely surrounded by snow-covered mountains. There was nothing within sight or hearing. We wondered why we had been taken there. Some high-ranking Swiss Army officers came over to the streetcars, told us to line up in front of them. One of them told us to follow him in single file; we started to go down a hill, and soon some old grey buildings came into sight. Since these buildings were below us, we hadn't seen them from the top. When we reached them, and entered, we couldn't believe our eyes.... there were two large rooms, and against one wall there were two-story high wooden platforms with straw on them. We had been promised we would be staying in nice hotels until we were to go to America, but this didn't look like a hotel; it looked more like the barracks we had just left. We didn't complain, but were very disappointed.

Soon an event happened that made us forget the uncomfortable quarters we had been given. The assistant commandant of the area came to our room, and told all of us to gather around. He made a short but frightening speech. He told us that the American consul was coming that afternoon to interview everyone personally and that those without the proper papers would be sent back to

BERGEN-BELSEN. After all we had been through, after all the suffering, when we were so overjoyed to be free again, to have our hopes and dreams smashed! We couldn't believe what we had heard. After all, it had come from a man with authority. We hoped that he was wrong.

To take my mind from what I had just heard, I went outside to talk to one of the Swiss soldiers who was on guard duty, complete with rifle. He was only 14 years old. He told me that this building had been a school twenty years before, then converted into a horse stable, and about a year before, was made into a camp for Swiss soldiers. I noticed the kitchen and went there, where I found four soldiers working. They were very friendly and I was happy that I had learned to speak German; otherwise, I would not have been able to talk with them. One boy, who was an Italian, had fled from Italy three months before when the Germans tried to arrest him and send him to Germany. Another 17-year-old boy, German, swam across Lake Constanz to Switzerland, as he could not in his heart fight against Americans. When he arrived in Switzerland, the Swiss government had put him to work in this camp, because they didn't allow undocumented foreigners to walk around freely. The chef came over to me and asked if I wanted to help out in the kitchen. I was happy to do so, as I didn't know how long we would have to stay, and it wouldn't hurt to be near food. So I worked in the kitchen, and enjoyed it very much, and learned a lot in those few days about cooking, especially for large amounts of people. There were other benefits to this job; the chef gave me extra food every night, such as milk, butter and cheese, which I shared with my mother. The others in our camp weren't as lucky, as there was a food shortage in Switzerland and everything was rationed. Generally, the food was good, and we all got as much as we wanted.

The next morning the American consul came, just as promised by that "diplomatic" officer the day before. He was a well-dressed, likable gentleman. He asked if anyone in our group could speak English, to translate what he had to say. My mother volunteered, and I was so proud of her.

She and the consul had a long conversation, and I could tell by her expression that he was telling her what she wanted to hear. When he left, my mother translated what he had told her. We did NOT have to go back to Bergen-Belsen, nor did he plan to give us an interview. He apologized that we had to live under these conditions, but the hotels were filled to capacity with people who had fled from war-torn countries. We wouldn't be here long, and would be leaving any day now. After that, we wrote my father a letter, telling him the good news.

We began to wonder why we hadn't heard from him yet. He had always written to us; even when we were in the camp, he would write my mother notes almost daily. That afternoon my mother had to go to the hospital in St. Gallen, because she was still feeling very weak. I went to see the Swiss commandant of the camp to ask permission to phone my father in the hospital, because I was so worried about him. He agreed, and assigned one of his soldiers to guide me to a nearby store, as the one phone in the camp could only be used for military purposes. We walked for about an hour through the mountains in the snow until we reached a small village. There we entered the post office, which was also the local headquarters for the Swiss Army. My guide went over to an officer sitting behind a desk, and told him that I had received permission from the commandant to make a phone call to the hospital where my father was. He had to call the operator for me, as I didn't know how telephones worked there and, although I knew how to speak German, the Swiss spoke it with an entirely different accent.

After a wait of ten minutes for the connection to the hospital, my guide handed me the phone and I felt nervous. A nurse asked me who I wanted to speak to. I told her that my father was a patient in that hospital, where he had been taken two days before, when we had left Germany. She told me to wait a few minutes, and would try to get him on the phone. Those few minutes seemed like hours, and when she finally returned, she told me that she was very sorry the doctor would not allow my father to come to the

171

phone. I asked about his condition, she told me that he was doing well, but I didn't believe her. Tears came to my eyes as I hung up the phone. Then my guide told me to come along, and we started our journey back to the camp through the beautiful scenery, but I didn't notice any of it; my mind was elsewhere.

That evening, my mother returned from St. Gallen, where the doctors had given her some medicine and advised her to rest as much as possible.

Two days later, January 29th, 1945, is a day I will never forget. The morning started the same as it had for the past three days. I worked in the kitchen, making some soup for that afternoon's dinner. In the afternoon, the chef told me that I didn't have to work, as we were going to have a cold supper. My mother and I took a nap to catch up with some sleep we had lost during the past few hectic days. At four o'clock, we were awakened because the commandant wanted to see the two of us outside immediately. We hurried to get dressed and went outside, where we were met by the commandant and an aide. By the sad expressions on their faces, I knew something was wrong. He asked my mother if she was Mrs. Spanjaard and if I was her son, Barry. When we told him we were, he said, "I am sorry to have to tell you this, but your husband just died in the hospital."

I can't describe my feelings at that moment. I just stood there, stunned. My mother started to cry and I held her in my arms, and brought her inside with me. The others had heard our tragic news, and came over to pay their respects. It was nice and thoughtful, but it didn't help. After I brought my mother some water, and a few women came over to her, she quieted down and spoke softly, "Oh, this is terrible! Think of it, two years in a concentration camp, and after he is free for only three days, and finally on his way back to America, he had to die. He wanted to live so much, to take care of us again, because he couldn't for so many years." She started to cry again, and it took us a long time to quiet her down. It was a terrible shock to both of us. That night neither my mother or I got much sleep. Every time I managed to fall asleep, her crying would wake me. At first, I tried to console her and asked her to stop crying, but then I knew it would be best to let her cry. I felt it was my responsibility to be strong and hide my grief, but the pain has never left me.

The next morning some officials from the Swiss government came to see us and promised that they would return with a car to drive us to the hospital, to attend my father's funeral. The day before we had received nice clothes and shoes, and we would be properly dressed for the ceremony. They also asked us if we needed anything, but we told them we didn't. At least my dad would have a decent burial, not like so many thousands of others who had just been piled on top of one another, then dumped into mass graves. I was thankful for that.

The day of the funeral, the commandant came to our building at 5 A.M. to awaken all of us. He told us to pack, as we were going to leave for America. Here we were, being told to get ready to leave for America; yet, we were supposed to go to my father's funeral. My mother went to see the commandant and reminded him about my father's funeral, scheduled for that morning. He said that he was sorry, but he had received orders from the American authorities that no one was allowed to stay behind for any reason whatsoever. The only thing left for us to do was to pack our few belongings.

An hour later we were told to report outside with our baggage. As we left the camp, we each got a paper bag with our lunch, consisting of a couple of rolls and a cold hot dog. This time we went uphill. It was a bitterly cold morning, which is unusual for Switzerland. When we reached the top, we found the same streetcars that had taken us there a few days before, but we had to wait about an hour before they let us enter them. Waiting there, my thoughts were with my father, who was probably at that moment being laid to rest, all alone, without his family. When the commandant saw me crying, he came over and said that he was so very sorry that my father could not go with us, and wished me much luck. We entered the streetcars, and left. At St. Gallen station we found a long train waiting for us. It was a pleasant ride clear across the country; the scenery was gorgeous, but I couldn't appreciate it. I began to miss my dad, and every mile took me further and further away from him....

Showing my American pride to Hitler Youth. Germany — January, 1945

175

DADDY'S GRAVE IN MUENSTERLINGEN,
SWITZERLAND
"Victim of camp Bergen Belsen.
Your strength lasted until entering free ground.
You witnessed the premature end of
6 million Jews in the years 1933-1945"

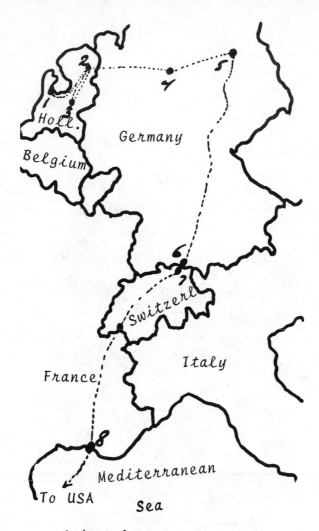

1. Amsterdam
2. Westerbork Concentration Camp
3. Amersfoort Concentration Camp
4. Bergen-Belsen Concentration Camp
5. Berlin, capital of Germany, where
   150 civilians joined us.
6. Konstanz, on Swiss-German border
   where exchange took place.
7. St. Gallen, Switzerland near
   where my father is buried.
8. Marseille, France, where we boarded
   the Gripsholm for return
   to U.S.A.

XIII. THE FENCES COME DOWN—GATES OPEN

It took exactly five hours to go from one end of Switzerland to the other, where we stopped in a beautiful, large city. I didn't know where we were, so I asked one of the Swiss soldiers standing on the platform. Naturally, I asked him in German, but he didn't understand me. Then I remembered from school that they speak three different languages in Switzerland. I knew that we were on our way to France, and probably now in the French-speaking part of Switzerland. So, I asked the same question again, this time in French, and got an answer: we had arrived in Geneva. It was 5 o'clock in the evening, and for a change, we again had to wait. The train had ten cars. At 7 o'clock they started to transfer us to a nearby hotel, starting with the first car. It was three hours before we were taken to the hotel where we had soup, bread, and a few apples for dinner. It turned out that we were not to stay there, they had just taken us for dinner, so when we got through eating, we went back to the train.

The station at Geneva was really two stations, divided in the middle by a gate. One part was in Switzerland, and the other in France. We were told to take our luggage from the train, as we were to walk across the border into France. I then got a thrill, seeing real American soldiers. I had seen them in action, had seen them fly over us so many times, and had even seen them getting captured; and here they were, standing right in front of me.

A pullman train was waiting for us on the French side of the border, and we continued on our journey about midnight. What made this part of the trip so interesting for me was that this time our hosts were American officers. They came and talked to us to see how we were doing. My mother, who spoke perfect English, could talk to them. They were sincerely concerned about our welfare. I felt left out because I couldn't talk to them myself.

Soon it was time for our first meal in France, and what I remember most was the bread. It was pure white, the first white bread I had seen. It was so soft, I couldn't believe it was something you could eat, I thought it was cotton. My mind was still always on food, and impatiently waited for each meal.

After a long ride through Southern France, which had been recaptured by the American forces, we arrived in Marseille about ten o'clock that night. The train pulled up onto a large pier, with a large ocean liner on each side. A few minutes after we arrived, American Red Cross women boarded our train and handed out donuts, coffee and hot chocolate.... *real* coffee, and *real* hot chocolate. I had never seen a donut in my life, as we didn't have them in Europe. Very carefully, not really knowing what it was, I took a small bite, and liked the taste so much that I ate 36 of them. The women, from whom I kept taking them, looked at me rather strangely, and I am sure they thought I was some kind of animal.

After a few hours' wait, my mother and I were told to get off the train. We were brought into a quonset hut, where we saw well dressed civilians sitting behind tables. They impressed me with their nice haircuts, clean white shirts, ties, beautiful suits, and I thought they were all American millionaires. We were thoroughly questioned and asked for our papers. Two questions stand out in my memory: "Where is your husband, Alfred Bernard Spanjaard?" And, "Where is Mrs. Elizeba Spanjaard-Groen?" my grandmother. My mother told them that my father had died a few days before in Switzerland, and my grandmother had been killed in the gas chambers in Poland. We were told my grandmother would have been allowed to accompany me, a minor American citizen, to the United States. After the questioning, when they checked that our papers were in order, we were led onto one of the ocean liners, a Swedish ship, The Gripsholm. Sweden was a neutral country, so the American authorities hoped the Germans would let this ship cross the Atlantic without attacking it.

After boarding the Grispholm, my mom and I went to our assigned cabin. It was small with bunk beds, and I slept on the top. As soon as we entered, I became violently ill and threw up, the result of eating those 36 donuts. I then fell asleep; and at eight the next morning was awakened by the cabin steward, because it was time for breakfast. Even though I was still exhausted after only four hours' sleep, and not recovered from my battle with the donuts, when the man mentioned "food," I jumped out of bed, got dressed, and ran to the dining room. My mother was not feeling well, and told me to go ahead and enjoy myself.

The dining room was a large formal salon. I was particularly impressed with all the white tablecloths, something I hadn't seen in a long time—it was dazzling. I was then led to a table set for four people and sat down. It soon became apparent that the other three people, one of them my mother, were not joining me. I was given a menu by the waiter, but I couldn't read it, as it was in English, I just pointed to something, not knowing what it was. Then I pointed to the three empty chairs at the table, and somehow managed to get across to the waiter that I was asking him where the other people were. He shrugged his shoulders as if to say, "I don't know." After much hand-motioning, I somehow conveyed that he might as well bring me their breakfasts as well. As a result, my first American breakfast consisted of: 4 glasses of orange juice, and 4 portions of bacon and eggs. I had never seen bacon, and eggs were unavailable to me for almost five years. I had now been out of Bergen-Belsen for nine days, and as far as food was concerned, I was still like an animal who was afraid that anytime someone would come and take it away from me, and never would I have this kind of food again.

I felt my strength coming back, and after this enormous breakfast, decided to explore the ship. I looked for some of the people who had come with us from Bergen-Belsen, but couldn't find them. All I could see were American military men, who were badly wounded. Some were blind, some had no arms or legs, many had burned faces and others walked on crutches. I found out later that there were about 550 men, or I should say BOYS, since most of them were about 18 or 19 years old. They had all been prisoners of war, and most of them had been shot down over Germany. The Germans had exchanged them as these men were in no condition to fight again.

Once in a while I would see former P.O.W.'s who had apparently nothing wrong with them, had arms and legs, were not blind, and with no burn scars on their faces. A few days later when I saw some of them in the swimming pool, I knew why they too had qualified for exchange; I saw one whose entire right shoulder had been shot away, and another who was severely burned over his entire body except for his face.

My mother told me, after she had spoken to some of these men, that there were 63 who had been placed in the mental ward of the ship, suffering from total battle fatigue.

As there were no first, second or third classes, I had the complete run of the ship. I still couldn't find any people from our camp. I mentioned this to my mother, so she went to speak to the men in charge. She was told that all the others from our camp did not have the correct papers. They had been put on the other ship across the pier from us, and were to be sent to a camp, called Phillipsville, in North Africa, until the end of the war. So, it turned out that my mother and I were the ONLY ones from Bergen-Belsen who were to actually go to the United States on this transport. We felt sorry for the others, but were to meet some of them in New York shortly after the war.

The American soldiers were continually smoking, as they had been deprived of cigarettes for a long time, and now were able to get as many as they wanted. I saw that some of them would take a few puffs, and then put the cigarettes in the sand-filled ashtrays. This, in my young mind, seemed a good opportunity to make money. Now that my stomach was full, I could start thinking about how to become "a rich American millionaire." Assuming that cigarettes were scarce in America, I could make a "fortune" selling the tobacco left over from these hundreds of cigarette butts. I carefully collected as many as I could find, took the tobacco out of the papers, and accumulated several boxes full of tobacco. Towards the end of the trip, one of the soldiers aboard saw what I was doing, and asked me in broken German, what I was doing. I explained my plan, and after he stopped laughing, he told me that I was wasting my time, as there was no serious tobacco shortage in the states. I had now failed in my second business venture, the first one was my "sour" milk concession in Amsterdam.

On another one of my excursions through the ship, I found myself in back of one of the kitchens, where they stored the food. (By the way, we were still tied to the pier in Marseille, and how long we were going to be there, no one knew.) I saw a stack of canned powdered milk, and many crates of fresh oranges, things I hadn't seen in a long time. I took as many cans of milk under my shirt as I could fit, and as many oranges as I could fit in my pants' pockets. I was still under the impression that I would never be able to get these things again, so I wanted to be prepared. I carefully walked through the hallways back to my cabin, so as not to get caught.

My mother told me that they were going to show a movie on the ship, called "The Sky is the Limit," starring Fred Astaire, whom I had never heard of. Though I was fifteen years old, I had never seen a full-length movie in my life, only cartoons and newsreels. Before the war, once in a while my dad took me to the "Cineac" theatre, in downtown Amsterdam, where, for ten cents, you could see cartoons and newsreels for an hour before one o'clock in the afternoon. I went to see this movie, but the trouble was that it was in English, and I couldn't understand it, and felt very frustrated. Here I was, an American-born boy, and I couldn't even understand my "own" language. This same feeling of frustration was also with me whenever I was in the company of those fine American soldiers. I was aching to talk to them, to find out where they were from, how long they had been in Europe, how long they had been in P.O.W. camps, and how and where they had been captured. It must have been the same for them, as they had not seen a young boy in a long time, and they too would have liked to talk to me. I remember how impressed I was that most of them, in spite of their injuries, managed to have fun and laugh. Laughter had not been a part of my life for a long time, and Europeans seemed more serious. These Americans all had such a great sense of humor.

One day I found myself surrounded by a group of soldiers who had taken an interest in me. I'm sure that they were wondering what the hell I was doing there, but they seemed to like me anyway. One of them put his arm around me and said, "Hey, kid, where is your big sister?" They all laughed, and I was certain he had said something dirty. When I asked my mother what it meant, she said they had meant no harm and "were just curious about my family." Of course, a few months later I realized what they *really* wanted.

I enjoyed hanging around them, as they were a lot of fun, so, one day, a few of them said they were going to teach me English. My first lesson consisted of learning how to say, "Go to hell!" I didn't know what it meant, but I didn't really care. They kept rehearsing me, and after a while, they wanted to see if I had learned my lesson, so they gave me a test. (All this time I thought "go to hell," was some sort of greeting, like "how do you do.") A large man, wearing an impressive uniform, smoking a big cigar, entered the room; and my "teachers" gently pushed me in his direction, whispering the recently learned phrase in my ear. I walked over to him, and proudly said, looking him straight in the eyes, "Go to hell!" He looked at me rather strangely, while the men who had sent me on this mission were laughing their heads off. What I didn't know was that the man I had "greeted" was a two-star general. So much for my first English lesson.

The first time they showed "The Sky is the Limit," things about the movie puzzled me greatly. I saw buildings with signs, "VACANCY." In Dutch, the word "vacantie" means vacation, and I could not figure out why people in America would advertise with signs on their homes that they were on vacation. The movie was shown six times, and I went every time. First of all, I didn't have anything else to do beside stuffing myself at mealtimes, and I thought this might be a good way to learn English. Each time I saw it, I would pick up a few phrases and a few words. So, Fred Astaire, indirectly, became my first English teacher.

We spent an entire week in the harbor of Marseille. One afternoon while I was on the deck, observing the activities on the pier, I noticed that the other ship had left, I assumed for North Africa.

I saw men playing, and observed two new things. Some of them had black skin, which I had never seen before. They were throwing an oddly-shaped object back and forth. It was shaped like an egg and must have been a ball. The only kind of balls I had ever seen were round balls used in soccer and basketball. I just figured that because of the war this was the only thing they had to play with. Another possibility was that their ball had been run over by a truck, causing it to flatten out. Some time later, I discovered that it was an American football. Then I couldn't figure out why it was called a "football," when in fact, it was rarely kicked.

I was awakened one morning by vibrations from the ship's engines.... we were finally on our way. It was hard to believe that we were actually going to the United States. It took a couple of days to go through the Mediterranean Sea, which was very smooth. An announcement was made when we reached the Straits of Gibraltar that we were entering the Atlantic Ocean. Immediately, the ship started to bounce around, and quite a few people got seasick. It took two weeks to cross the Atlantic, which normally would take one week, as we had to continually zig-zag in order to avoid mines.

A frightening thing happened one night. A siren was sounded, and we were told to put on life jackets and report on deck. Once we got there, I saw the ship completely lit up with spotlights, and the Swedish flag hoisted. Rumors quickly spread, the most consistent one was that a German U-boat had spotted us and was about to torpedo us. The reason for this show of colors was to make the Germans aware that we were neutral. The U-boat was quite close to us, and I could clearly see its periscope before it surfaced. There was a stand-off for about a half hour. Suddenly, the submarine submerged, the "all clear" was sounded, and the lights went out again. An announcement was made that all was safe and we could return to our cabins. How easy it would have been for the German submarine to sink this totally unarmed ship with heavily wounded American soldiers and hundreds of helpless civilians. The captain of the submarine must have received orders from his superiors that this was an exchange mission and not to attack us.

The rest of the voyage was pleasant. My mother and I talked about how wonderful it would have been if my dad was with us, looking forward to our arrival in New York.

After our three weeks on the Gripsholm, February 21, 1945, an announcement was made on the public address system that we were about to enter New York harbor. My mother and I ran to our cabin to pack our belongings, which consisted of one outfit of clothing and shoes each given to us by the Red Cross. We did not realize that we didn't need to hurry, as we were to spend another THREE days on the ship, before we were allowed to disembark.

Our arrival in New York harbor was a spectacular event. Many boats of all sizes surrounded our ship to welcome the returning G.I.'s as heroes. When we slowly passed the Statue of Liberty, almost everyone on board started to cry; it was quite a sight. That whole day made a tremendous impression on me. Just as April 6th, 1943, changed my life for the worse, this day was to change my life for the better. I saw one young G.I. who couldn't have been more than 20 years old, with only one arm, guiding his blind buddy, onto the deck. The blind boy said, "Hey Mac, do me a favor; when we pass the 'old lady' (Statue of Liberty) in the harbor, will you let me know?"

Everyone on board was on deck, standing on the side that was to pass the statue. The captain made an announcement that since this was the end of the journey, without the weight of fuel, food and water, the ship was light and high out of the water and listing very dangerously, and to please spread out over the entire ship.

It was all very exciting. More boats approached us, some were fire boats spraying water. Small planes flew over with signs saying "WELCOME HOME" flowing behind them.

Ever so slowly we came closer and closer. My first view of the lower part of Manhattan was overwhelming; I had never seen such tall buildings, and my thoughts went back to Bergen-Belsen when my mother told her campmates about this. Now it was all real; now I was here, seeing it with my own eyes; it was unbelievable, and a lump came in my throat.

A tugboat pulled up with civilians who boarded the Gripsholm. Another came near with a loudspeaker blasting: "Don't Fence Me In," sung by Bing Crosby, in honor of all the G.I.'s who had been prisoners. One soldier standing next to me said to another: "This can't be New York... the Krauts told me that they had flattened it."

At 12:30 we docked at Pier "F" in Jersey City, New Jersey. A large military band was playing on the dock, and a group of military brass boarded the ship as the excitement mounted. Thousands of people were standing on the pier, waving frantically, screaming, smiling, jumping up and down trying to locate loved ones they hadn't seen in a long time, most of whom, they felt they would never see again. Some were carrying large signs with names of returning soldiers on them.

When things had quieted down a bit, there was an impressive ceremony held on the top deck. Several generals pinned Purple Heart medals on the chests of the returned war heroes. Then quite a few men were carried on deck, whom I had not seen before. These were the very seriously wounded, who could not move around at all. On one stretcher lay a boy, no older than 19, with no legs and only one arm. As soon as he appeared, a colonel ran over and hugged him... They talked and smiled; it was a "happy" reunion. The colonel then called over another officer, and I heard him say, "General, I want you to meet my son."

Soon they started to move the men on stretchers from the ship, and once that was completed, the rest of the returning G.I.'s left, to be greeted by many tears and many open arms. I wonder what became of all these wonderful guys, my "first English teachers" ... If only my dad could have been here with us to share our happiness.

My mother was looking for her two sisters and brother whom she had not seen in 13 years, who were living in New York. She had written them before leaving Bergen-Belsen. She didn't see them, and found out later that they had not been allowed to come to the pier. Only relatives of returning soldiers were permitted for security reasons.

By the time all the soldiers had disembarked, it was 8 P.M., and we were told that no one else would be allowed off, as the custom and immigration officers had gone home. We were very disappointed, but hoped that the next morning, we would all be allowed to leave. We were thoroughly questioned by the Federal Bureau of Investigation, and for good reason. Among the civilians who had boarded our train a few weeks ago in Berlin, Germany, were spies. German Intelligence had given them fake birth certificates and passports in order to have them included on this exchange trip. The F.B.I. caught them all.

My mother and I were questioned on several different occasions. After the first session, we were very disappointed that we were not allowed to leave. Here we were so close, perhaps ten feet away from American soil, and yet so far away. The F.B.I. knew so much about us. I was even questioned about a Dutch Anti-Nazi song I sang to my G.I. friends. They wanted to know what the song was about and called in another agent who could speak Dutch. I sang the song for them. When I got through, the agent nodded his approval.

After three endless days of waiting, we were finally allowed to leave. A Red Cross stationwagon took us into New York City, through the Lincoln tunnel, which they told me, was built by Dutch engineers. The tunnel seemed to take forever, and when we reached the exit, I got my first glimpse of New York City, that famous city my mother had told me so much about. She smiled through her tears, as now her fondest wishes and dreams had come true; she had returned to her love, her New York, and said, "Barry, you are now in the city you were born."

We arrived at our destination, the Red Cross Headquarters building at 38th Street and Lexington Avenue in Manhattan. There we were met by several relatives who had been waiting there all this time. My mother's twin sister, Bep Sammes, her husband Jo, my mother's older sister, Zeddie, her husband Jacques, my mother's brother, Maurice with his wife Cora and daughter Rita. I had two more cousins; cousin Flos was in the Navy in Washington D.C., and my cousin Jackie was in the Army, somewhere in India. So much family, all at once, was totally overwhelming. An uncle of my father, the one he had worked for in New York many years before, was also there, and wanted to take me home with him, but the rest of the family said no, I was to go home with them. I would visit him later.

Here I was, back in the land of my birth, unable to speak its language, fifteen years old, without a father, literally a stranger in my own country. I set my goal to learn English, become Americanized, and complete my education. Most important of all, I would try, if possible, to forget the past few horrible years, and look forward to a new future in this land, where I could finally be FREE...

THE BEGINNING

"Go to Hell!"

FEDERAL BUREAU OF INVESTIGATION

Form No. 1 THIS CASE ORIGINATED AT NEWARK, NEW JERSEY			FILE NO. 108-523 CAM	
REPORT MADE AT NEWARK, NEW JERSEY	DATE WHEN MADE 3/16/45	PERIOD FOR WHICH MADE 2/22/45	REPORT MADE BY	69C
TITLE ABIGAEL SPANJAARD, nee Abigael Rooseboom, was Abigael-Roosebaum, Abigail-Roozeboon, Sophie. Spanjaard Rooseboom, Sophie Rooseboom; BARRY ALFRED SPANJAARD, Passengers MS GRIPSHOLM, Arrived Jersey City, New Jersey February 21, 1945.			CHARACTER OF CASE FOREIGN TRAVEL CONTROL	

SYNOPSIS:

ABIGAEL SPANJAARD born November 30, 1901 Amsterdam, Holland and is not a United States citizen. BARRY SPANJAARD born August 16, 1929 in New York City. ABIGAEL resided in United States 1921 to 1932 and returned to Holland for business reasons. Both passengers resided in Amsterdam until April 6, 1943 when interned at Camp Westerbork in Holland and in Camp Bergen Belsen. Released for repatriation to the United States January 21, 1945. ABIGAEL's husband died in Switzerland January 29, 1945 after release from internment camp. Subject intends to reside temporarily with friends in Brooklyn, New York. ABIGAEL SPANJAARD will seek employment as a nurse or secretary. BARRY will attend school.

- C -

REFERENCE:

Bureau letter dated February 5, 1945 entitled "Incoming Passengers MS GRIPSHOLM Arriving Jersey City, New Jersey About February 20, 1945 - FOREIGN TRAVEL CONTROL."

Teletype from Newark to New York dated February 13, 1945.

Letter from New York to Newark dated February 17, 1945.

APPROVED AND FORWARDED:	SPECIAL AGENT IN CHARGE	DO NOT WRITE IN THESE SPACES	
		108-1273-1	RECORDED & INDEXED

COPIES OF THIS REPORT
5 - Bureau
1 - Col.S.V.CONSTANT,SID,2SC (CONFIDENTIAL)
1 - Capt.T.S.KING, USN,DIO,3ND (CONFIDENTIAL)
1 - New York (Information) COPY IN FILM
3 - Newark

EX-41

MAR 29 1945

Official F.B.I. report of our interrogation,
obtained through the Freedom of Information
Act

NX 108-523

DETAILS:

ABIGAEL SPANJAARD and BARRY ALFRED SPANJAARD arrived at Jersey City, New Jersey on February 21, 1945 on the MS GRIPSHOLM on the sixth repatriation voyage from Marseilles, France. They had been interned at Camps Westerbork and Bergen Belsen. Their repatriation was arranged by the United States Department of State. They were interviewed by Confidential Informant T-1 and the writer.

PASSENGER QUESTIONNAIRE

ABIGAEL SPANJAARD executed a passenger questionnaire on February 14, 1945 in which she stated that her last permanent address was Amsterdam, Holland and that she was proceeding to J. VAN STRATEN, 105 Lincoln Road, Brooklyn, New York. Her date of birth is shown as November 30, 1901 in Amsterdam, Holland and she is a citizen of Holland. Her marital status is widow. She indicated that she speaks, reads and understands English, French, German and Dutch languages.

She further stated that she had attended elementary and high schools in Amsterdam, Holland from 1907 to 1916 and that her usual occupation is that of housewife. In regard to her special skills or scientific training she indicates that she is a registered nurse and a reporter.

She also indicated that she has been in the following countries:

                1901 to 1921 in Holland
                1921 to 1932 America
                1932 to 1943 Holland
                1943 to 1945 concentration camp in Germany.

She stated that she does not own any property in the United States or in any foreign country. She has never been arrested for any crime but was fingerprinted in Amsterdam, Holland in 1941 by the German authorities. Her purpose for coming to the United States is to accompany her son who is a United States citizen. She did not furnish the names of any references in the United States and stated that she did not have any military or naval information which might be of interest to the United States Intelligence officers.

A passenger questionnaire was also executed by BARRY ALFRED SPANJAARD in February 14, 1945. This form contains substantially the same

- 2 -

192

information as contained on the passenger questionnaire executed by his
mother. He indicates, however, that he was born August 16, 1929 in
New York City, is a citizen of the United States and has never lost his
citizenship by expatriation or otherwise. His marital status is single.
He cannot speak or understand the English language, but does speak, read
and understand Dutch, German and French. He attended elementary and high
schools in Amsterdam, Holland from 1935 to 1943.

PERSONAL HISTORY STATEMENT

A personal history statement was executed by ABIGAEL SPANJAARD
and in addition to the information shown on her passenger questionnaire
contained the following information. Her name at birth was SOPHIE ABIGAIL
ROOSEBOOM and she is in possession of a Dutch passport number 153319 which
was issued in Amsterdam, Holland. She also has a birth certificate issued
in Amsterdam, Holland and a certificate of marriage issued in 1927 at New
York City.

Her father's name is NATHAN ROOSEBOOM and her mother's
WILHELMINA SUGET both residing in Amsterdam. She lists the following as
her two sponsors in the United States: JAKE VAN STRATEN, 105 Lincoln Road,
Brooklyn, New York and HENRY POLAK VAN OVERVEEN, 1705 Eaton Avenue, Long
Island, New York.

A personal history statement executed by BARRY ALFRED SPANJAARD
indicates that he is in possession of birth certificate number 27036 issued
by the New York Board of Health. He indicates on this form that his father
is ALFRED BARRY SPANJAARD and his mother SOPHIE ABIGAIL ROOSEBOOM. All
other information is contained in his passenger questionnaire.

INVESTIGATION PRIOR TO ARRIVAL

The following investigation was conducted by Special Agent
██████████████ of the New York Field Division: b7C

Mr. JACQUES VAN STRATEN, reference, residing at 105 Lincoln
Road, Brooklyn, New York, who is an executive of Loew's Theatres, Inc., 1540
Broadway, New York City, advised that the passenger, SOPHIE SPANJAARD, nee
ROOZEBOOM, is the sister of his wife, ROSETTE. He stated that she was born

- 3 -

193

in Amsterdam, Holland on November 30, 1902, and first entered the United
States for the purpose of living with him and his wife in New York City,
sometime in 1921. Mr. VAN STRATEN further stated that his sister-in-law
resided with them until 1932. He said that from 1924 to 1926 she studied
to be a nurse at both the City and Metropolitan Hospitals, located on
Welfare Island, New York City. She was married to BERNARD ALFRED SPANJAARD,
a native of Holland, in New York City in 1927, and their only child, a son,
BARRY, was born on August 16, 1929. Mr. VAN STRATEN advised that Mr.
SPANJAARD for several years was employed in the banquet department of the
Waldorf Astoria Hotel, and at the Hotel Astor, New York City. He stated
that they returned to Holland in February of 1932 because Mr. SPANJAARD
inherited his father's real estate and antique brokerage business. VAN STRATEN
stated that he and his wife corresponded regularly with the SPANJAARDS until
the Germans occupied Holland, but that since that time he advised that they
have only received two letters from Mrs. SPANJAARD, and these were very brief
messages transmitted through the American Red Cross. He stated that in
her last communication, Mrs. SPANJAARD said that they would probably be
interned by the Germans, inasmuch as their son, BARRY, was an American citizen.

He stated that he heard nothing further concerning their
activities until when reading the "New York Times" on February 6, 1943,
he learned that BERNARD ALFRED SPANJAARD was reported to have died in
Switzerland. The next information he had, Mr. VAN STRATEN advised, was
received from the State Department, notifying him and his wife, that SOPHIE
SPANJAARD, and her son, BARRY ALFRED SPANJAARD, were coming to the United
States aboard the MS GRIPSHOLM. He further advised that arrangements have
been made to care for the passenger and her son as soon as they are allowed
to leave the vessel, and he expects both of them to reside at his home at
105 Lincoln Road, Brooklyn, New York. He stated that he and his wife were
very sad to learn of the death of Mr. SPANJAARD, since they regarded him
very highly, but were overjoyed with the news that Mrs. SPANJAARD and her son,
BARRY, would soon be with them again, and he stated that he was sure that
she expected to remain in the United States permanently this time and become
an American citizen, since BARRY is a native born citizen.

VAN STRATEN furnished the following names of close relatives
of Mrs. SPANJAARD: BERTHA SALLES (twin sister), 7401 Ridge Boulevard,
Brooklyn, New York; MAURICE ROOZEBOOM, Overlook Terrace, New York, who operates
the Holland Rubber Company, brother, and LOUIS ROOZEBOOM, Le Perreux, Paris,
France, another brother.

Mrs. SAUL BENJAMIN, Hotel Granada, Brooklyn, New York, stated
that she was born and grew up in Amsterdam, Holland, and all her life has
been a close friend of the passenger, SOPHIE SPANJAARD, and has always known
her family. She advised that the passenger is a very fine woman, and although
she has not seen her since she returned to Holland about thirteen years ago

- 4 -

194

with her husband and infant son, still she had no hesitancy in recommending
her as a person well qualified to live in the United States.

At the Hotel Astor, New York City, Mr. I. P. VAN DYKE,
assistant manager, advised that BERNARD ALFRED SPANJAARD was employed as
a clerk and typist in the banquet department of that hotel from September
17, 1928 to January 2, 1930, and was reemployed from February 15, 1930
until September 19, 1931. He did not recall this employee, but contacted
the managers of the banquet department, ROBERT D. HOWARD, and Mr. GARNIER,
who recalled SPANJAARD. These two individuals were unable to furnish any
information regarding BERNARD ALFRED SPANJAARD's citizenship status, but
stated that they had never heard him make any derogatory remarks against
this country, nor had they ever heard anything that would reflect on his
character. They recalled that SPANJAARD, while employed there had requested
a raise in his salary because of the birth of a child to him and his wife.
They both said that SPANJAARD was very obliging and industrious, and well
regarded.

The records of the Marriage License Bureau, Municipal Building,
New York City were checked, and reflected that BERNARD ALFRED SPANJAARD,
age 24, was married to SOPHIE ROOZEBOOM, age 25, at New York City on
October 31, 1927. In the application for the marriage license, SPANJAARD
indicated that he was born in Amsterdam, Holland was employed-as a salesman
residing at 101 West 89th Street, New York City. His parents were listed
as BERNARD SPANJAARD and EVA GROVER SPANJAARD, both born in Holland.
SOPHIE SPANJAARD stated that she was born in Amsterdam, Holland, and was
employed as a cashier, residing at 168 West 85th Street, New York City.

The records of the Bureau of Vital Statistics, New York City,
reflect that BARRY ALFRED SPANJAARD was born in New York City on August 16,
1929 at the Polyclinic Hospital.

The indices of the New York Field Division were checked with
negative results.

In addition, the indices of the Newark Field Division and of
the Bureau were checked for information regarding these subjects with
negative results.

<u>INTERVIEW</u>

Upon being interviewed ABIGAEL SPANJAARD advised that she had

resided in the United States from 1921 to 1932. While residing in this
country in New York City she met ALFRED BARRY SPANJAARD and married him in
New York City on October 31, 1927. She had in her possession a certificate
of marriage showing that on this date SOPHIE ROOSEBOOM was married to ALFRED
B. SPANJAARD. She also had in her possession her birth certificate showing
that ABIGAEL ROOSEBOOM was born on November 30, 1901 in Amsterdam, Holland,
the child of NATHAN LEVI ROOSEBOOM and WILHELMINA SUGET. She stated that
her son, who was traveling with her on the GRIPSHOLM, was BARRY ALFRED
SPANJAARD.

She produced a certified copy of the birth certificate
number 27036 issued by the New York City Board of Health showing that BARRY
was born on August 16, 1929. She advised that in 1932 she returned to
Holland with her husband and son because her husband's father had died and
her husband had gone to Holland to take over his father's antique business.

At the time of leaving New York City the family had resided
at 501 West 167th Street, New York. On arriving in Amsterdam they resided
at Amstelhade 10 from 1932 until their internment by the German authorities
in 1943. She stated that during this entire period of time she called at
the American Consulate in Holland and had her son registered as an American
citizen. She stated that both she and her husband were citizens of Holland
and had never become naturalized United States citizens during the period of
residence in New York City.

Regarding her internment by the German authorities, she advised
that the Germans had called on several occasions but had not interned them
inasmuch as BARRY was an American citizen. She stated that they were frequently
abused because they were Jews and finally on April 6, 1943 she and her husband
and BARRY were taken to Camp Westerbork, which she described as a camp where
persons were ordinarily held only to determine the future camp to which they
would be sent. They were held at this camp until May 18, 1943 when they were
sent to Camp Anursfoort where they were held for one month and returned to
Westerbork on June 20, 1943.

On February 1, 1944 the family was transferred to Camp Bergen
Belsen where they remained until they were released for repatriation to the
United States on January 21, 1945. She indicated that at these camps they
were cruelly treated and that her husband was frequently taken out and
beaten for no apparent reason. She stated that it was due to these beatings
that her husband died on January 29, 1945 in Switzerland while he was on his

- 6 -

196

way to Marseilles, France to be repatriated. She also pointed out that she was never asked if she wanted to go to the United States or to Holland but that the camp commander at Camp Bergen Belsen came to her one day and asked her if she wanted to go to American and when she stated she would he told her to get ready in ten minutes.

She advised she is not carrying any messages, either written or oral for any person presently interned in any camp in Germany. At the time of her interview she had approximately $65 in her possession and stated that she intends to secure employment in New York City. She pointed out that she has had experience as a reporter and also claims to be a registered nurse in New York City, having taken the nurses' examination in 1922 and 1923 and at one time was employed as a nurse at the city hospital on Welfare Island, New York City.

She stated that she was also qualified to hold the position of a secretary. She intends to go directly to her sister's house, ROSETTE VAN STRATEN at 105 Lincoln Road, Brooklyn, New York, but will probably not live there permanently as she desires to be independent. She can, however be reached through this address at any time.

INFORMATION ON OTHER PASSENGERS

The passengers stated that they could not give any derorgatory information concerning any crew member or passenger on board the MS GRIPSHOLM or any person presently interned in a concentration camp in Germany.

BAGGAGE SEARCH

The baggage of the passengers was searched with negative results.

DISPOSITION

At the conclusion of the interview the passengers departed the MS GRIPSHOLM for the home of Mrs. SPANJAARD's sister, Mrs. ROSETTE VAN STRATEN, 105 Lincoln Road, Brooklyn, New York, where they will temporarily reside. Mrs. SPANJAARD stated that she can always be reached through her sister.

from the internment camp her weight was approximately 75 pounds to 80 pounds.
At the time of the interview her weight was approximately 110 pounds. The
passenger also stated that she would have the remainder of her teeth extracted
as soon as possible and secure false teeth which would probably change the
contour of her face. Her fact at the present time is very thin but is
normally quite fleshy.

Relatives
Sister, BERTHA SALLES, address
unknown, Brooklyn, New York
Brother, MORRIS ROOSEBOOM, address
unknown, New York City, business
Holland Rubber Company
Sister, ROSETTE VAN STRATEN, 105
Lincoln Road, Brooklyn, New York
Cousin, LOUT H. MICHAELS, 165-20
Highland Park Avenue, Jamaica,
Long Island, New York
Cousin, HENRI POLAK VAN OVERVEEN,
1705 Coton Avenue, Brooklyn, New
York
Uncle, HENRY A. GROEN, 550 Fifth
Avenue, New York City.

THE FAILURE TO DEVELOP ANY DEROGATORY INFORMATION AS A RESULT
OF THE INVESTIGATIVE EFFORT OF THE FEDERAL BUREAU OF INVESTIGATION, A PERSONAL
INTERVIEW OF THE PASSENGER OR A CHECK OF ITS FILES DOES NOT CONSTITUTE AN EN-
DORSEMENT OR APPROVAL OF THIS PASSENGER'S ADMITTANCE OR ENTRANCE TO THIS
COUNTRY BY THE FEDERAL BUREAU OF INVESTIGATION.

- C L O S E D -

- 9 -

198

These are Identical Twins

This is What the Nazis Did to One

Pages 8-9

Front page picture of my mother and her twin sister as it appeared on April 22, 1945, in the "P.M." a New York City newspaper.

Back in New York - 1945

Back in Germany - 1953

Jacques and I; still best friends.

Telling my story to students; my life's work.

"THIS IS YOUR LIFE" Barry Spanjaard

(shown on the N.B.C. - T.V. network on January 28 and July 14, 1984)

L to R: Martha Vance Ellisor, former liaison officer from the Red Cross' Gripsholm crossing (from Newberry, S.C.) - Steffany Jantzen, an appreciative former high school student who heard me speak in 1982 - my camp buddy and boxing partner, Jacques G. (specially flown in from Israel) - host Joe Campanella - me - my Uncle Joe (from Puerto Rico), hadn't seen him in 23 years - my best friend and wife, Bunnie (driven in from Canyon Country) - my favorite son Fred, and Betty C. an old family friend who has known me since I was three years old (flown in from Holland).

202

EPILOGUE

Most of my dreams about the United States did come true, but as opposed to fairy tales, we did not "live happily ever after," I had the normal ups and downs.... I moved in with my Aunt Zeddie in Brooklyn, while my mother went to live with her twin sister. The doctors found me to be in good physical condition, amazingly. Even though I hadn't been able to brush my teeth in two years, all they needed was a good cleaning. I was given a private tutor and learned English quickly, and then attended P.S. 210, John Marshall Junior High School in Brooklyn, and during the summer vacation I went to a Boy Scout Camp.

My mother spoke professionally for the United Jewish Appeal, and was responsible in raising millions of dollars for thousands of Displaced Persons left in Europe to settle in Palestine, until 1948. She regained her health and strength and blossomed during this exciting time because she was involved with something worthwhile. Being highly respected, she met important people from the political and entertainment fields all over America. She was a dramatic and effective speaker. When I attended some of her speaking engagements, I was very proud of her.

In the meantime, I was sent to a military school in Virginia. Feeling abandoned by my family, I could not figure out what I had done to deserve this kind of punishment as I again was in a situation where men in uniform were in complete control of my life.

In 1946, after my mother had finished one of her lectures at a women's club in Brooklyn, a woman approached her, who was also Dutch, and invited us to dinner. My mother said I was away at school, but would be home for Christmas vacation, and we would then be happy to accept her invitation. When we entered her apartment, I was shocked to see a picture of my old girlfriend, Ellie R., who I had assumed to be dead. It was her niece, who had survived with her brother by hiding with a Christian family in Holland; in fact, she was still living with them, as her parents had been exterminated. I wrote Ellie a long letter, and visited her a few years later in Holland. She is now married, has five children, grandchildren, and lives on the East Coast of the U.S. No, she did not marry me.

It was years later that we found out what really happened to my cousin Norbert. During the war between France and Germany, his plane had been shot down somewhere over France. He managed to bail out and landed near a Catholic convent, where the nuns kept him hidden from the Germans. He remained there until the end of the occupation. When the war was over, and my cousin was free to go, he was so grateful to the nuns, that he studied for the priesthood, and was ordained in 1948.

In 1950, my mother became an American citizen, something she had always desired and she took great pride in her new status.

After Palestine became the State of Israel, in 1948, my mother's services were no longer required by the United Jewish Appeal. This sudden removal from the public arena, and the feeling that she was no longer needed, caused her to go into a deep depression. She attempted suicide, was institutionalized, and under psychiatric care for years, all to no avail. In 1961, after another suicide attempt, it was decided by the court and the doctors that she could no longer function in the outside world. She remained in a large New York City mental hospital until her death in May of 1977.

In 1951, after saving money from jobs as a shipping clerk, and a trainee in Wall Street, I went to Europe to see who was left of friends and family. The first stop was to my old apartment in Amsterdam, where we had been arrested. It was a traumatic experience. Strangers, now living there, were nice enough to let me in. I entered, looked at my bedroom, our living room and my parent's bedroom. I cried as thoughts of happier days came back to me.

I also went to see our upstairs neighbor who, together with my Dad, had hidden my Bar Mitzvah rings. He told me he was sorry, but he couldn't remember where they had buried them. What was I to do? Get mad? Force a confession from him? I put myself in his place. That last winter in Holland was brutal, they were hungry, cold, sick and miserable. Here was this small treasure belonging to a Jew who had been shipped off to a concentration camp, and who ever heard of a Jew coming back from such a place? So he probably traded them with farmers for food. Perhaps, inadvertently we saved his life.

I had a happy reunion with my best friend from the camps, Jacques G. He, his mother and one brother had survived; his father, his oldest and youngest brother all had died within one week, immediately after the liberation of Belsen.

During the Korean War, I was drafted. Of all places, they sent me to Germany as a member of the United States Army Forces of Occupation, and assigned to Military Intelligence because of my knowledge of German. Ironic isn't it? The Army did not know of my camp internment or they would have thought twice about giving me an opportunity to walk around Germany with a loaded rifle. There were many occasions when I had to practice great self-control among Germans who I thought looked "familiar."

I married a New York Jewish girl in December 1952, and she followed me to Germany, where we got a little apartment in Mannheim. On May 12th, 1955, our son Fred was born, in Heidelberg, Germany, in an American Army hospital. While stationed there, on one of my leaves, I traveled to Switzerland and finally got the opportunity to visit my father's grave. Thoughtful members of the Swiss Jewish Community had seen to it that he had a nice headstone. They placed a memorial placque by his grave, honoring those who had been murdered by the Nazis.

After my discharge from the service in September 1955, I worked as a buyer's trainee in a large New York City department store, while driving a taxi at night and on weekends. One afternoon, an elderly gentleman got into my cab, and when he read my Dutch name on my taxi license, asked me where I had been during the war. I told him that I had been in the camps. His eyes saddened when he asked me if by chance I had known his little girl, Annie in Belsen.... He was Otto Frank, Anne Frank's father.

In 1959, my wife, my son Fred and I moved to Los Angeles, California. Neither of them or our friends knew much about my childhood. This marriage ended in divorce in 1968. In 1971 my lucky day came when I met my wife-to-be, Bunnie. She encouraged me to add to the original manuscript written in 1946, to expand on it, and retype it, after she carefully corrected the many misspellings and grammatical errors.

As the sun sets over the Santa Clarita Valley, we are trying to "live happily ever after"....

Canyon Country, California
September, 1981

I envied boys who had grown up in this free country, their clean clothes, their uninterrupted education, their cars, their boy-girl relationships, who played ball on the street after school.

They had grown up in nice, peaceful neighborhoods, had friends, and were able to maintain these friendships for many years. Most of MY childhood friends were gone.

I envied boys with four grandparents, the Jewish boys who had festive Bar Mitzvahs, with all their loved ones there, with no worries about being "caught," because they were doing something illegal.

I envied boys who had both parents. I wondered if they ever thought about these things, or did they take all this for granted, something they had coming to them?

I still shudder whenever I hear a teenager say, "Man, am I starved, let's get a hamburger." Of course, he doesn't know the *real* feeling of starvation, and I hope to God he never will....

Retail $9.95

SPECIAL DISCOUNTS

Students, teachers, libraries - 20% . . . . $8.00 each

Class sets (minimum 25 copies) - 40% . . . . . $6.00 each

Shipping Charges Included
Consignment Orders Accepted

TEACHER'S GUIDE

$2.00 each - FREE WITH BOOK ORDERS OF 25 OR MORE

FOR LARGER QUANTITIES, CONTACT PUBLISHER

RECOMMENDED BY THE
NATIONAL EDUCATION ASSOCIATION

UNITED STATES
HOLOCAUST MEMORIAL MUSEUM SELECTION

FOR SPEAKING ENGAGEMENTS,
PLEASE CONTACT:

B. & B. PUBLISHING
P.O. Box 800165
Santa Clarita, California 91380
TEL (805) 255-3422
FAX (805) 254-1404